SACRED RETREAT

"The minute I started reading this book, I got chills. My body said a big 'yes' to this information. Yours will too! Every mother and every daughter should read this book."

CHRISTIANE NORTHRUP, M.D., AUTHOR OF
MOTHER-DAUGHTER WISDOM, *THE WISDOM OF MENOPAUSE*,
AND *WOMEN'S BODIES, WOMEN'S WISDOM*

"We simply cannot secede from nature, and to believe otherwise is madness. Orleane shows how we can remain in nature's flow and reap the benefits that are a part of this inescapable oneness."

LARRY DOSSEY, M.D., NEW YORK TIMES BESTSELLING
AUTHOR OF *ONE MIND*

"This gentle, deeply reflective book offers us another way of seeing the world—through the eyes of feminine vision. With penetrating insight, it recovers for us a long lost wisdom and offers a template of how we might restore balance to our driven, radically unbalanced society and our stress-filled lives. Anyone reading *Sacred Retreat* will have their understanding of life deepened and enhanced, leading them into a more conscious way of living, a closer relationship with their body, and an interweaving of their life with the rhythms of the natural world, the planet, and beyond that, the cosmos. A hugely valuable book."

ANNE BARING, AUTHOR OF *THE DREAM OF THE COSMOS*

"Orleane's well-documented and well-written book is full of wisdom. An antidote for these fractured times, it is a call for us to return to the natural wisdom of our bodies, to reclaim our innate power, and to reconnect with the cycles of the natural world."

ERICA ELLIOTT, M.D., PHYSICIAN, SPEAKER, AND
COAUTHOR OF *PRESCRIPTIONS FOR A HEALTHY HOUSE*

"Pia Orleane, Ph.D., is a talented researcher and writer with a feel for people and their lives. I strongly encourage you to consider her book. Here is a strong, unusual, and inspiring study valuable for many. Pia helps open magic to us."

RUTH RICHARDS, M.D., PH.D.,
AUTHOR OF *EVERYDAY CREATIVITY*

"*Sacred Retreat* gets to the root of the current planetary crisis and how we can transform it. This book is an accessible and practical guide to bringing the feminine back online by starting with our own bodies and cycles. I immediately put the insights from this book into practice and felt richly rewarded with increased intuition and empowerment. Any woman or man who desires to realign with the rhythms of nature will receive great benefit from the practical wisdom offered here."

EMILY TRINKAUS, AUTHOR OF
CREATING WITH THE COSMOS

"Pia Orleane, Ph.D., writes with passion and conviction. *Sacred Retreat* is an antidote for the stress and depression so prevalent in today's tattered cultures."

STANLEY KRIPPNER, PH.D., COAUTHOR OF
*EXTRAORDINARY DREAMS AND
HOW TO WORK WITH THEM*

"Every day we witness the great imbalance in the world that our current story and ways of living have brought us. This book offers an insightful guide on how humanity can return again to balance. Pia Orleane's book is a profound instruction manual."

MARIANNE MARSTRAND, EXECUTIVE DIRECTOR OF
THE GLOBAL PEACE INITIATIVE OF WOMEN

"*Sacred Retreat* is not only an important book, it is vital for humanity! Every mother should put this book in the hands of her sons and daughters. Every teacher should teach from this book in schools all over the world. And war would end. This is a vibrant book with important wisdom for both men and women. The divine feminine is sending the message to change NOW!!"

ERIKA MIKAELSSON, JOURNALIST AND
CEO OF NORDIC LIGHT MEDIA

"Pia Orleane, Ph.D., well deserves the accolades she has received for her original research, much of which is eloquently expressed in her unique comprehension of the natural cycles of life, especially as it relates to women and the reclamation of the divine feminine. This unique, informative, and process-oriented book is greatly needed to empower women and rebalance the current patriarchal dominance the world over."

NICKI SCULLY, AUTHOR OF *SEKHMET*

"Throughout the world, there is a real problem with gender inequality and our relationship with Mother Earth. These are challenging times and we need people that can give us wisdom and hope in the struggle. Orleane does just this in her book *Sacred Retreat*. Everyone wishing for social change and peace in the world should read this excellent book."

ROY BOURGEOIS, FORMER CATHOLIC PRIEST AND FOUNDER OF
SCHOOL OF THE AMERICAS WATCH (SOA WATCH)

"Pia Orleane has made an important contribution to the growing recognition of the importance of feminine values in our unbalanced society. This book provides a desperately needed corrective to our growing malaise and is well worth reading. It offers immediate practical and ultimately spiritual suggestions for both women and men."

GUS DIZEREGA, PH.D., AUTHOR OF *PAGANS & CHRISTIANS: THE PERSONAL SPIRITUAL EXPERIENCE*

"An invaluable reminder to get our lives back in sync with the undeniable wisdom of Nature—including our own physiological, emotional, and spiritual rhythms and synchronicity with all beings with whom we share and co-create our world."

ADAM GAINSBURG, AUTHOR OF *SACRED MARRIAGE ASTROLOGY* AND FOUNDER OF SOULSIGN.COM

"The power of Orleane's writing has far-reaching implications as modern women continue their ancient Earth cycles during these tumultuous times. In a readable and completely fascinating way, we are brought to reconfirming ourselves as vessels of wonder and awe."

EMILIE CONRAD, FOUNDER OF CONTINUUM MOVEMENT AND AUTHOR OF *LIFE ON LAND*

"This rich, timely work clearly rises from the depths of a woman's soul. It is, indeed, an invitation into life's mystery. This work is a 'must' for all those who seek the healing of the human condition."

KENNETH HAMILTON, M.D., AUTHOR OF *SOULCIRCLING*

SACRED RETREAT

Using Natural Cycles to Recharge Your Life

PIA ORLEANE, PH.D.

Bear & Company
Rochester, Vermont • Toronto, Canada

Bear & Company
One Park Street
Rochester, Vermont 05767
www.BearandCompanyBooks.com

Text stock is SFI certified

Bear & Company is a division of Inner Traditions International

Copyright © 2017 by Creative Wave, LLC

Portions of this book are based upon the author's previous publication *The Return of the Feminine: Honoring the Cycles of Nature,* published by AuthorHouse in 2010, and her 2001 Ph.D. dissertation, *Empowering Women through Sacred Menstrual Customs: Effects of Separate Sleeping during Menses on Creativity, Dreaming, Relationships, and Spirituality*

All rights reserved. No part of this book may be reproduced or utilized in any form or by any means, electronic or mechanical, including photocopying, recording, or by any information storage and retrieval system, without permission in writing from the publisher.

Note to the reader: *The information contained in this book is intended to educate, delight, and expand your understanding. It is not intended to diagnose or treat any medical condition, nor is it intended as medical advice. If you have concerns about your health, please consult with a health care professional.*

Library of Congress Cataloging-in-Publication Data
Names: Orleane, Pia, author.
Title: Sacred retreat : using natural cycles to recharge your life / Pia Orleane, Ph.D.
Description: Rochester, Vermont : Bear & Company, [2017] | Includes bibliographical
    references and index.
Identifiers: LCCN 2017013556 (print) | LCCN 2017030611 (e-book) |
    ISBN 9781591437918 (paperback) | ISBN 9781591437925 (e-book)
Subjects: LCSH: Medicine—Philosophy. | Mind and body. | BISAC: BODY, MIND &
    SPIRIT / Spiritualism. | SELF-HELP / Spiritual. | BODY, MIND & SPIRIT /
    Inspiration & Personal Growth.
Classification: LCC R723 .O75 2017 (print) | LCC R723 (e-book) | DDC 610.1—dc23
LC record available at https://lccn.loc.gov/2017013556

Printed and bound in the United States by Lake Book Manufacturing, Inc.
The text stock is SFI certified. The Sustainable Forestry Initiative® program promotes
sustainable forest management.

10 9 8 7 6 5 4 3 2 1

Text design and layout by Virginia Scott Bowman
This book was typeset in Garamond Premier Pro with Trajan Pro, Gill Sans, Pro and
Hypatia Sans Pro used as display typefaces

To send correspondence to the author of this book, mail a first-class letter to the author c/o Inner Traditions • Bear & Company, One Park Street, Rochester, VT 05767, and we will forward the communication, or contact the author directly at **www.piaorleane.com.**

Contents

✽

Foreword
Barbara Hand Clow

I HAVE WRITTEN much about the cycles of change, and in this wonderful book Pia Orleane, Ph.D., has gone deeply into the divine feminine. We are linked in some mysterious way. Considering some cosmic cycles of change that affect Earth; the most significant Mayan Calendars ended in 2011/2012; the Age of Aquarius is dawning; and we have just completed seven revolutionary squares between Uranus and Pluto (from 2012 to 2015) that exploded human society by creating a whirlwind of radical change. These transformations will play out until the new planetary structures emerge that will work for individuals and society in the coming era. Uranus rules revolution and Pluto rules transformation, so the seven squares between them have decimated mass belief in the patriarchal paradigm of the last five thousand years. Yet, entrenched male control has not yet released its stranglehold because each one of us needs to banish dominance from our homes and communities.

Most of us know we must eliminate these outmoded forms, yet we struggle with how to do that. I think this is because we don't collectively know where we are going. Orleane's book offers a compelling way to reestablish male/female balance, which we will need for survival while the patriarchy—poisoned by disproportionate materialism and militarism—staggers and falls. In *The Mayan Code,* I hypothesize we are evolving into *Homo pacem,* "man of peace." Whatever we will become, the one thing we know for sure is we will not survive the great transition without attaining harmony within our families and with our planet.

While I've considered the great changes of this era, I have also traveled into humankind's deep past to reflect on what it was like to be human over the last one hundred thousand years. What must come forth in the near future will emerge naturally out of the remarkable accomplishments that have brought us to this point. The creative complex of the future draws us ever forward because it is sourced in our origins. To gather wisdom from the deep past, one must find ways to experience archaic worlds. I have done this extensively by using past-life regression under hypnosis to write my trilogy, *The Mind Chronicles: A Visionary Guide into Past Lives.* And I still experience archaic worlds in my ordinary life with the modality known as ecstatic trance, as developed by the anthropologist Felicitas Goodman, Ph.D. Both of these practices allowed me to travel into the Paleolithic and Neolithic worlds, as well as into more recent historical phases. But these practices are demanding and occult. Delightfully, in this book, Orleane describes a more accessible practice for reweaving modern consciousness with our deep past. Known as the sacred retreat process, it involves women choosing to seclude themselves when they are experiencing their menstrual period so they can purify and evoke new creativity in tune with the cycles of the moon and the stars.

This practice pulls men and women right back into harmony with the deepest elements in their psyches by accessing the rhythms of nature and blood. This simple and very ancient ritual allows women and their partners to end discomfort and judgment around the monthly "curse," which Orleane calls "Nature's gift." By transforming Nature's gift into a cleansing process that awakens new creativity, it becomes a cyclic renewal that partners can actually look forward to. While a woman goes deep within and balances herself with the moon and the night sky, her partner gives her the retreat space that all women so terribly need. Orleane believes, as I do, that women are inherently more powerful than men because they bring children into the world; their monthly bleeding is a potent reminder of this power.

Determined to seize power five thousand years ago, the patriarchy and later, Christianity, demeaned women's bleeding. This incursion upset male-female balance, which then has resulted in ecological destruction. Orleane implores us to adopt a woman's seclusion while she bleeds to bring harmony back into our lives, which will then naturally reestablish nature's harmony. If couples, including same-sex couples, choose respect for the masculine and the feminine, then militarism, the patriarchy, and ecological abuse will miraculously dissolve.

Orleane's book is deep, all-inclusive, and very evocatively composed. You can hear her voice calling out for balance. She tested the efficacy of the book's mandate in the research projects she undertook with couples, as described in appendix 1, and she has surveyed global blood rituals and taboos in appendices 2 and 3. I found myself wanting to test her results against the vast stretches of time I've traversed, since the great cycles I've already described are converging now. We are in the middle of adjustments in contemporary cultures that can abolish old negative patterns forever, but many people feel paralyzed. Given that harmony between the feminine and masculine is the fundamental basis of human society, everyone—male and female alike—needs to rebalance these patterns. During the convergence of cosmic cycles, we need bonding and self-reflection to benefit from radical transmutation.

Going back into the end of the archaic phase when we first became conscious of ourselves in nature—an emerging process we observe in cave art going back more than forty thousand years—imagine the mystery people felt when women bled. Women had to seclude themselves for contemplation. The universality of this tradition observable in the remaining hunter-gatherer and indigenous people suggests that seclusion of women who are bleeding goes back to our first emergence.

During the Neolithic, we became more conscious of our individuality, as can be seen in artifacts and art from this period. Women became fascinated with the power they felt when they bled; they intuited that it led to their being able to give birth. They used this secluded time to build upon this sense of power by developing themselves as leaders, healers, and teachers. In those days long ago, women and men were equal. Even though my monthly cycles ended many years ago, I still remember the day I first bled: I went deeply into a state of magical contemplation because I was overwhelmed by the awareness that I could one day have a child.

Following the Neolithic came the dominance of men over women. This began five thousand years ago. During this patriarchy, women were demeaned so that men could seize their power. This false move overemphasized the differences between them and the subtle male/female nuances eroded. A growing lack of respect for the positive benefits of monthly bleeding and birthing transformed a woman's power base of fertility into the woman's curse. These days this distortion is so extreme that people are confused about their gender identity. Of course! It was taken away from them!

It's my belief that Orleane's sacred retreat process, which includes how men can recover the benefits of andropause ("male menopause" wherein a drop in testosterone and other hormonal changes occur), can restore gender clarity—the fundamental basis of healthy human fertility. Orleane notes that this practice is still an aspect of Muslim and Jewish spirituality, and that the sacred retreat process is mainly lacking in Western Christian culture. Ours is a destructive society in which science markets artificial insemination and conducts research to create test-tube babies. Needless to say, manufactured and genetically engineered babies would be the ultimate triumph of the patriarchy.

In any event, the imposition of the patriarchy created militarism, sexual abuse, and the erosion of the fertile family, the great scourges that torture us today.

Orleane's simple idea, the return to deep contemplation based on our fundamental biological functions in tune with nature's cycles, could bring us slowly back into male/female harmony. With the recovery of that exquisite joy—living in the heart with our partners—the next stage of our evolutionary form can emerge easily and safely. When the great ages shift, the old world must dissolve, which is difficult for some and traumatic for most. We boil in our blood when we see terrified refugees streaming across the sea and land. We cringe when we see mothers, fathers, and children running away from bombs and soldiers. We despair when we see millions of homes being blown to bits. We must have peace in our homes while going through this long-awaited transition into a new era.

Orleane offers a simple and practical way to achieve this aim. This wise book shows us how to use the natural wisdom of our bodies to return to harmony with nature, the path to the future. I find that this book holds great potential to change the world.

BARBARA HAND CLOW is an internationally acclaimed ceremonial teacher, author, and Mayan Calendar researcher. Her numerous books include *The Mind Chronicles, Awakening the Planetary Mind, The Mayan Code, The Pleiadian Agenda, Alchemy of Nine Dimensions, Catastrophobia,* and *Astrology and the Rising of Kundalini.* She has taught at sacred sites throughout the world and maintains an astrological website, www.HandClow2012.com.

Opening Remarks
Cullen Baird Smith

IN HER NEW BOOK, Pia Orleane, Ph.D., has created a blueprint for understanding the importance of the nature of cycles that control and ultimately influence all of human life. Her book is not only timely but also provides a necessary message to help society reach higher levels of consciousness.

We have reached a place where it is fundamentally impossible to regain any kind of social balance without combining the positive attributes of the divine feminine with those of the divine masculine. All of the feminine aspects of life have been denigrated and abused by the patriarchy for far too long. This new book can help us to make better, more conscious choices to benevolently survive, prosper, and evolve. And it will certainly take reestablishing respect for the divine feminine to lead us in this timely and critical direction.

Orleane's groundbreaking research and work has the potential to rebalance the gulf between the genders and to restore our lost equilibrium through the power of the divine feminine. Her novel approach to the issues at hand is more relevant and necessary at present than it has been at any other time in human history. The wisdom and principles of which she writes so eloquently can help all of us return to and respect our innate abilities to listen to and utilize deep intuition in a more direct fashion. The wisdom contained in her work can actually make a significant change in the world.

Humanity has been severely out of alignment with nature and natural cycles for a very long time. One of the principles that Orleane's insights bring to us is the understanding that we *are* nature. We have, however, moved further and further away from nature by adhering to the dominance of a patriarchal, linear world view. This off-centered approach to life has taken us away from our natural abilities to deeply listen to and trust our own rhythms. Without honoring our human biological cycles, we are doomed to failure as a society, by continuing to make disconnected linear choices in a technologically governed, patriarchal system.

The patriarchy has literally gone mad with a one-sided attitude of dominance, aggression, and linear thinking that has spawned the maniacal and disastrous development of technologies that have nearly annihilated nature and the very existence of mankind. Technology speeds us up and prevents us from communicating deeply with each other, further separating us from the natural world that supports our biological essence. The patriarchal principles of conquering nature, as opposed to the feminine principles of cooperating with nature and her cycles, will continue to take us in the wrong direction. The information that Orleane imparts through her words and concepts has the potential to realign our planet with the ability to make conscious choices led by the divine feminine to help us to regulate and moderate the chaos we have collectively created over millennia. Without a fundamental respect for coherence with nature, there can be no stability in our lives. We are, indeed, nature itself.

This work is not only intended for women, it is an equally valuable and important resource for men as well. Men need the leadership of the divine feminine in order to rebalance themselves and society at large. Our culture has lost its connection to nature and natural cycles and must be brought back into balance to ensure the evolution and survival of humanity and the planet. We must all heed this critical message in order to slow down and to listen deeply to what the divine feminine has to share. It is time to make new and better choices if we wish to prosper and thrive together.

The principles that Orleane suggests have the power to release the tension between the genders by returning to a more natural understanding of the cycles that govern our human biological and emotional behaviors. She stresses the need to return to nature to encompass these universal truths. In fact, she implores us to return to nature, listen to our own intuition, and honor the natural cycles that govern our lives.

It is time to remarry the archetypes of the divine feminine and the divine masculine to create a more balanced world. By utilizing the tenets and practices brought forward in Orleane's new book, we can not only envision but also create a society that is balanced and egalitarian. If any force or energy is ever to support this much needed change, or if equilibrium is ever to be achieved, it must certainly be led by the wisdom of the divine feminine.

CULLEN BAIRD SMITH is a visionary, a seer, a sensitive, and an energy healer. Cullen has participated with non-ordinary states of reality since early childhood. Coauthor of *Remembering Who We Are: Laarkmaa's Guidance on Healing the Human Condition* and *Conversations with Laarkmaa: A Pleiadian View of the New Reality*, Cullen began facilitating the energetic healing of others when he was four years old. At age nine, Cullen produced a "Findhorn garden" in his backyard through a connection with the Devic kingdom, preceding the magical and renowned Findhorn Gardens in Scotland by a decade.

Acknowledgments

MY FIRST THANKS go to my heartmate, Cullen Baird Smith. As a balanced, spiritual man, he consciously carries the divine feminine within him more than most. Every day he shows me his longing to create a just world that is fair to all. Our intense and illuminating conversations about the imbalances in the world are reflected throughout this book. I am very grateful to him for encouraging me to publish this work and for the beautiful opening remarks he wrote for this book. These opening remarks reflect his wisdom and understanding. I am grateful for his sharing a few of his original terms for my use, and his valuable, critical eye, and editorial abilities. His edits allowed me to see what needed expanding or deleting and helped me to understand my limitations so that I could move beyond them. I also appreciate his having connected so lovingly with me on all levels and in all conditions. Thank you, Cullen, for seeing me, for believing in me, and for appreciating me. Thank you for sharing yourself with me, and for being my full partner in every sense of the word. What a joy to live with you! Our path together continues to be truly divine.

I am deeply grateful to Barbara Hand Clow for her encouragement to get this work into the world, for our shared understanding of the importance of natural cycles, and for the wonderful, supportive foreword she wrote for this book.

Thanks to Anne Baring, for her vision, her deep insight, her inspiration, and her support. Her suggestion to be true to my knowledge without being tentative encouraged me to use my feminine power to express myself.

I extend my ongoing appreciation to my longtime friend Rebecca Gretz, without whose technical support I would be totally lost. Thank you for so often helping me to research subtle points to gain a broader perspective. Your deep friendship, dedication to evolutionary growth, trust in the universe, and amazing approach to life make the world a better place!

Thanks to my good friends Diann (Sara) and Brendan Bowen for early edits of my work. Your sharp eyes and editorial skills made this a better book. Thanks to Dan Gretz for technical support and occasional research assistance. I thank Marcellus Davis for facilitating Internet communication for me, given my choice to be separated from the digital world as much as possible.

I thank all the people at Inner Traditions • Bear and Company who helped me bring this work into the world, including Jon Graham, Kelly Bowen, Manzanita Carpenter, Erica Robinson, Patricia Rydle, Jeanie Levitan, Blythe Bates, John Hays, and most especially my amazing editors Jamaica Burns Griffin and Anne Dillon—wizardesses full of intelligence, style, flow, and depth. I am very grateful for their touch on my work.

I thank Saybrook University for supporting my research and me as a person. I am grateful you chose me to receive the prestigious Gerald Bush Award for Original Research and Creative Solutions. I thank all the women and men before me who contributed their voices to the value of the feminine.

My deepest gratitude to the late Emilie Conrad, my friend and a true visionary whose wisdom of the body was immense. What she knew, we all should know.

A huge note of appreciation goes to those friends and colleagues who recognized the worth of my work and provided glowing endorsements because they believed it can make a difference in the world.

A warm thanks also to all the women who enthusiastically participated in my original research on treating menstruation as a sacred time. Without your dedication to the project and willing support, I would not have been able to make the scientific conclusions that aligned so nicely with my experiential wisdom.

Thanks to my mother, May Jo Wootten, who always told me I came from the stars and taught me that I am divine. Thanks to my dad, William Robert Finlay, who gave me unconditional love. I miss you.

I give special thanks to all who are listening to the call of the divine feminine, but especially to my spiritual sisters Diana Johansson, Rebecca Gretz, Diann (Sara) Bowen, Sulara James, Erika Mikaelsson, Maria Belknap, Oribel Divine, and Jai-La Visitor—divine women who have loved and supported me in innumerable ways every day that I have known them.

Thanks to all the men who each in your own way demonstrate how honoring the divine feminine within you can be a powerful force for positive change on our planet. Special thanks to my friends Marcellus Davis, Brendon Bowen, Brian MacIntyre, Brad Oliphant, Terence Neff, Genesis Young, Alexander Senchenko, Wolfgang Hoffman, and again, my own beloved, Cullen Baird Smith. I am sure there are more of you to thank who I am remiss in remembering here. To those I've unintentionally omitted I give my heartfelt thanks.

My most profound gratitude goes to all members of my spiritual family and my unnamed friends, from both the human and other realms, who support my work and me in countless ways. Thank you for being in my life. My heart recognizes and appreciates our connections! To you, I send all my love, light, and deepest appreciation.

Introduction

LIKE EVERYONE reading this book, I grew up in a patriarchal culture. Because of prevailing attitudes and beliefs, my connection to nature's cycles was eclipsed as I absorbed a cultural belief system that valued progress and competition highly. Even children's games were built on the idea of winning. As I matured, I began to feel very uncomfortable about the rules that governed all of my behaviors; I felt unable to be myself.

Sitting on the beach one day, I watched the waves come and go, listening to the rhythmic sound beckoning me to join my water to theirs. I began to remember that I was connected to the sea and to its tides. The rhythm of the lapping waves awakened in me the memory of the divinity of my own rhythms. I am a water being. I am connected to and part of nature, and there can be nothing more holy than the divine cycles within me that connect me to Earth and help me remember who I am. To bring our relationship with all life and with ourselves back into balance, we need to understand and respect these natural rhythms.

When we are born, water constitutes approximately 78 percent of our bodies, yet as we age this decreases to approximately 60 percent. The same salt water that makes up the sea makes up our blood. The rivers within us are connected to the rivers of Earth. The moon causes a tidal pull of water on our planet, and our own waters also follow a rhythm of natural cycles. It took me a long time, however, to figure all this out. I spent a lifetime hiding from what my body communicated about what it wanted or needed from a culture that did not support those needs. I grew up hiding my menstrual bleeding because society considered it dirty; in short, I was embarrassed to bleed.

How many modern women have been damaged by cultural insinuations and led to believe that they are dirty because they bleed? In my youth, if the topic of the fertility cycle came up, boys made fun of us girls, whose sensitivities were greater during menstruation. Girls were thought to be weak, imbalanced, and undependable. Boys, on the other hand, were believed to be strong and reliable. I learned very quickly from others around me that girls were less valuable than boys.

With the arrival of menses at the age of thirteen my body was racked with violent cramps every month, and I was told that was normal. My church attributed the physical pain to a direct curse that had been placed on women for leading men astray. There were no standards of care to investigate possible hormonal imbalances as being the cause. Additionally, my cycles were irregular, so I was often embarrassed by the abrupt onset of monthly bleeding. With jokes and disparaging comments from boys, I became one of millions of girls who desperately wanted to hide—whether I was menstruating or not.

As I matured, I discovered there was also a double standard about sexuality. Girls were encouraged to refrain from sexual intercourse until marriage, and those who didn't quickly received bad reputations. Being sexual was simply not acceptable for girls. Meanwhile, society encouraged boys to make sexual conquests. I grew up hearing "boys will be boys," a sanctioned excuse for inappropriate male sexual behavior. Men were excused from bearing any responsibility for their sexual actions, while women who engaged in sexual activity were called whores or sluts. The reigning religious myths demanded that sex (for women) was only for procreation and allowed only in the sanctity of a church-blessed marriage. Female sexuality was to be used as an act of service to man and to God because women, according to the Christian myth, were responsible for the downfall of man. Such dogma severely harmed the esteem and position of women.

Our belief systems are deeply impacted by what we have been told and what we have experienced. To heal and rebalance the obvious division between women and men, we must eliminate old ways of thinking and claim the fullness of who we truly are: divine women and divine men. We must look more deeply at the cultural assumptions that continue to resonate in our psyches. We must know, not believe, that our bodies (female and male) are clean and pure and that the gift of our sexuality is an opportunity to experience unity and connect with the Divine, not simply a biological imperative required to populate the Earth.

A new myth needs to be created based on the truth: Eve claimed the wisdom of her divinity and shared it with Adam so that both of them could experience divine unity. Body-based wisdom and sensuality arise from a connection to nature.

As I grew and matured, I eventually learned all this. And later in life, I would also learn more about the menstrual cycle and why it was deemed to be sacred by various indigenous cultures of the world. It could have special benefits, which included the custom of separate sleeping quarters for women during the time of their bleeding. I learned that these Earth-based women generally chose not to be around men or other non-menstruating women during menstruation. They stopped all daily tasks—such as cooking and childcare—to go to a lodge to meditate, make crafts, dream, or commune with other women who were menstruating as well. Men were excluded. This time was understood by women and men alike to be a special time of purification because the women were shedding blood, emotions, and thoughts that no longer served them, or indeed, the entire community.

Once I heard that indigenous women considered the time of bleeding to be a time of purification, my first reaction was that I was simply hearing the same judgments about women's uncleanliness from another source. Nevertheless, I decided to experiment by creating a sacred space of my own and separating myself from others when I myself was bleeding. When my next menses arrived, I abandoned my usual routine and moved into my own space to meditate and dream. With nothing of my daily routine to distract me, I had ample time to come face-to-face with my own shadow and with what was and was not working in my life.

As I sat alone with my thoughts, I was flooded with painful memories, associations, and assumptions about who I was as a woman. I found that rather than providing a respite from the responsibilities of daily living, the time alone made me more accountable for eliminating my fears about being a woman. I examined all the hurtful beliefs I had been carrying, and I discovered that not only were they false, they were manifesting in a way that was causing me to struggle to be true to who I really was. Month after month, I faced the shadows of my own thoughts about being a woman. I battled the underlying cultural assumptions that women are impure and are only valued because they bear children.

One night during a menstrual retreat, I had a very meaningful dream in my private space. In my dream I was told who I really was and what I was capable of. On that night, I realized I was connected to everything, and I felt *proud* to be a woman. On that night I learned that it is necessary to move old things out of the way in order to make room for the new. Finally, I understood that cyclical bleeding is the precursor to creation in many ways, and that I could re-create myself every month by letting go of everything that held me back from being my full divine self. I finally knew that this was the real purpose of having a monthly menstrual cycle!

At last it all made sense to me and in the ensuing months, I gained a better understanding of the right timing of everything. I also realized that creating a sacred time and space for purification and introspection is more difficult for men, who do not have a biologically arranged timetable to do inner work.

Because these realizations felt important for all of humanity, I embarked upon a five-year, scientifically structured research project. At the end of the study, I had produced statistically significant information. The Consciousness and Spirituality Division of my university presented me a prestigious award for thinking "outside the box," along with the doctorate in psychology that I had earned. I found it ironic that what was considered obvious to our indigenous ancestors was now considered unusual thinking to our modern-day culture!

During my five-year study, I voraciously read everything I could find on the fertility cycle, especially Earth-based cycles. However, almost all of the recorded information had been written by white male anthropologists. This was because indigenous people do not write about sacred things. As a result, the material had a patriarchal bias. To find the answers I was seeking, I broadened my approach by visiting and speaking with indigenous women. What I found enlightened me but also saddened me. (I share these experiences with the reader in chapter 5.) The divine feminine principles I uncovered in my research compelled me to honor the flow and connection of all energies. These values are present in both women and men, but we have lost touch with them because in our technologically oriented modern culture, we have forgotten that we are part of nature.

In this book I explore the natural cycles that define our lives, offer ways to heal our relationships, and beckon us to listen to the call of the divine feminine to return to nature. It is the divine feminine that upholds values of cooperation over competition, generosity over selfishness, and connection with Earth and each other. When we focus on everyday problems, we often lose sight of the gifts that come from the cycles of nature. For this reason, in this book I have used women's cycles as a primer to understanding our relationships with each other and with everything on Earth.

Each of us, regardless of gender, carries aspects of the divine feminine within us, reminding us of our wholeness. Men who are becoming aware that they have feminine aspects to their makeup as well as masculine traits can help us return to a state of harmony, for these men are awake to their own nature and are very aware of the extent to which humanity is out of balance. It is these men, in concert with the women who are increasingly listening to and reclaiming their own divine feminine guidance, who hold the power to change the world.

Most men, however, are so driven by the societal demand for progress that they rarely take time for rest or contemplation. Medical science documents an increasing prevalence of heart attacks, high blood pressure, adrenaline-driven weight gain, alcoholism, expressions of unbound rage, and inappropriate, aggressive behavior in men. Given this, how can balanced decisions be made? Further, with patriarchal values ruling most of the world, many women have also succumbed to the need for constancy and linear progress. They too are at risk of developing the same set of physical issues I've just mentioned. Many women, as my heartmate says, seem to be "in training to be men." We have ignored natural cycles in almost every aspect of our lives, therefore, our values have become aligned with progress at all costs.

Paying attention to, and realigning ourselves with, natural cycles can help to mitigate all of this. And the good news is that just as women have cycles, men have cycles, too. Later I explore the unrecognized cycles that men undergo. These cycles include what is deemed to be the male equivalent of menopause, called andropause—a little-known term. Modern management of women's cyclical differences has spread to a generalized treatment of women as being inferior to men, especially in the workplace where women are often professionally marginalized, as in the example of a highly accomplished woman being sent out for coffee while the "more important" male viewpoints are discussed in a meeting, or passing over a qualified woman for promotion because a man is available. Men's cycles may be completely dismissed or disregarded, forcing them into a cultural role of constancy that does not reflect the truth of their complex masculine nature.

If we are not in tune with our own rhythms, then we experience sharp and inappropriate breaks or alterations in our life's flow. This is expressed in many women as premenstrual syndrome (PMS), and in men as uninhibited rage that often turns to violence. In chapter 2, I suggest that PMS is a culturally induced condition resulting from the scientific dissection of physical and emotional events that occur during the fertility cycle and a suppression of women's emotional vision. The rampant expressions of masculine rage today most likely come from the same imbalances within male cycles. I posit that the power of menopause has been squelched through lifetimes of cultural assault on women's cycles.

We need to simply put aside all cultural demands that are not aligned with natural cycles. If we desire a better life, we need to allow the power of the divine feminine to show us the way.

The fact that cycles and certain properties of behavior have been segregated and assigned primarily to women simply reveals the unhealthy split that has occurred between men and women. *Wo-man* and *fe-male* are words used by Western cultures to define the feminine gender in relation to men. No word in English communicates the essence of being female, and this lack of nuanced language reflects an existing lack of understanding of feminine principles.

Nature has provided women with a reproductive cycle that causes them to experience the world in varied ways, according to the timing of their biological cycles. This means that women have a dualistic way of being in the world, as I articulate in chapter 12. In women, problem solving, meaningful dreams, creative inspirations, and the desire for connection in personal relationships all vary according to what phase of the fertility cycle they're in. Unlike men, women use both sides of their brains simultaneously, joining right-brained creative thinking to left-brained analytical thinking through the corpus callosum. The corpus callosum is actually thicker in women, enabling them to use both sides of the brain in a connective way.

These dualistic ways of experiencing life give women the ability to easily change viewpoints according to circumstances. This trait also brings the ability to see multiple perspectives at once, which is a great attribute for mediating differences in controversial situations. Because women have language and emotional centers in both hemispheres with a thicker corpus callosum to connect them, women can also be more sensitive to and affected by harsh words and criticism. Women who are aware of this sensitivity recognize the importance of choosing one's words carefully, giving them an increased aptitude for creating harmonious communication and peaceful resolutions to conflict.

In his definitive work *The Natural Superiority of Women,* the renowned British-American anthropologist Ashley Montague enumerates the many qualities that give women a substantial biological advantage over men. Yet we have collectively decided that these differences are inferiorities. Such cultural biases are imbedded at an unconscious level, and they affect everyone.

For all of these reasons and more, the divine feminine is now calling out to all of us—both women and men—asking us to align ourselves with nature once again, to heal the imbalances on Earth, to find our lost compassion for one another, and to return to a practice of living with unconditional love. It is essential that we heal the horrible separation from nature that is destroying our planet. The divine feminine is the voice in our hearts that whispers, or sometimes shouts, that we must cooperate, that competition is separating us from one another, that peace is more valuable than possessions, and that true justice honors the highest good of all. Cultural and religious dogma based on judgment and hierarchical systems of power that decide what is right and what is not do not serve us any longer.

It is no coincidence that this book has thirteen chapters. Thirteen is the universal number of completion and a sacred number to women. The moon makes thirteen cycles around the Earth per year. Most women have thirteen menstrual cycles per year. I present the stories and information in these thirteen chapters in a winding, encircling, all-encompassing way—the way that the divine feminine manifests here on Earth.

In this book I stress the importance of women's biological cycles to show both women and men how honoring nature's guidance can strengthen our intuition, give us more opportunities to clean up the shadow in our personality, heal from our mistakes, improve our creativity, and deepen our relationships. There is no more poignant place to seek understanding of our place and purpose on Earth than to explore the mystery of cycles of life. In these pages I explore the similarity of feminine nature to all of the cycles of life. Like the gravitational pull of the moon that affects our inner waters, we are continually changing. Each change brings a gift and a different view of the world.

All things in nature move in cycles, and these cycles define life and death on Earth. A simple observation of nature shows cycles in the rotation of the Earth, or in tree rings that indicate yearly growth patterns. The scientific knowledge of life cycles expanded in 1729 when it was discovered that the *Mimosa pudica* plant exhibited a cycle when it closed its leaves at night and opened them during the day. Even as science explored the cycles of life, one of the most obvious and important life cycles, that of women's bleeding, has been pushed underground by the rules of our time. I explore the reasons that women's cycles have been ignored, dismissed, or pathologized, how men's cycles have been unrecognized, and how those actions have affected men and women, preventing us from being who we truly are.

In chapter 7, I show how culturally we have moved away from nature into a disconnected, technical approach to living that is stressful because it is out of harmony with our natural biological needs. This artificial way of living has thrown our most important relationships out of balance, even endangering future life by aligning our lives with technology over nature. Rather than appreciating the benefits of women's cycles, like the ever changing dark and light of the moon, we have been encouraged to design our lives according to a political calendar that artificially pressures us into a linear, progressive model of life— appointing nights, weekends, and holidays as the only sanctioned times for rest, regeneration, and introspection.

Unlike the modern Gregorian calendar that programs times of rest, calendar consciousness was first developed by women; it was based on their natural menstrual body calendar. Chinese women established a lunar calendar three thousand years ago; the words for "menstruation" and "calendar" are the same in the Gaelic language. Mayan women as well saw a relationship between the great Mayan Calendar and women's cycles, for they understood how energy cycles. Despite the ancient recognition of a woman's natural cycle and the benefits to the whole community, modern society has chosen to ignore or to manipulate the organic cycles of nature.

When I was young, American television was full of commercials targeting women that proclaimed, "Now you can be active every day of the month!" Messages like this helped promote the erroneous expectation that every day in a woman's monthly cycle should be the same. Not acknowledging our cyclical way of being isolates women from biological processes that occur anyway. Detachment from bodily changes ensures that those changes remain in the realm of the physical, thus bypassing the possibility of intuitive, creative, and/or emotional benefits being derived from them. Correspondingly, the necessity of a natural rest cycle for men has also been disregarded.

In chapter 6 and in appendices 2 and 3, I explore myths and beliefs of blood mysteries from the earliest times. I share the practices of people who live in harmony with nature (Earth-based people) to help move us beyond our limitations and allow us to be inspired by a model of a better life. People who live close to nature observe that life consists of interconnected processes. Through this understanding, Earth-based people acknowledge and respect the natural changes of women, unlike their mainstream counterparts.

Feminine principles are central to our homes and our communities; women are the natural creators of life. When women's cycles are ignored, controlled, or denied, there are far-reaching harmful effects, not only for women themselves, but for all of us as we detach from nature. Ignoring or suppressing women's natural cycles contributes to the increase of stress and illness, the deepening of sadness and depression, and greater separation in relationships.

Patriarchal misconceptions have imprinted themselves into women's consciousness as the truth. But all too often, patriarchal thinking is linear. It is concrete, rigid, and stifling; it blocks us in and paves us over. In contrast, the divine feminine moves in spirals that incorporate new information moment by moment, and changes accordingly. The energy of the divine feminine is fluid, flexible, creative, and nurturing.

It is time to heed the call of the divine feminine and heal our relationships, all of them, through living in harmony with nature. In the following pages, I show you how we can bring the qualities of the divine feminine back into our lives to heal our relationships and our world.

1

The Cyclic Nature of Life

WHEN YOU WERE A CHILD, did you spin and spin in a circle until you fell down, laughing uncontrollably all the while? Intuitively, children know that life cycles, and they instinctively follow that circular flow. Children aren't the only spinners. Sufi mystics whirl in a frenzied dance to achieve an ecstatic union with their God. Spinning is also the first of the Five Tibetan Rites, reported to stem from a Buddhist practice more than twenty-five hundred years old. Joy rises in those who flow with life.

All of life cycles. Everything is interwoven into a living system of cycles, from Earth's seasons to the enzymatic pathways that provide energy to a cell. Life is a process that waxes and wanes. Cycles of life are systematic, and balance is maintained by the nature of the cycle.

Cycles map the most auspicious time for everything in life. Birds know when to fly south for the winter. Dolphins use the cycles of the tide to determine when to search for food and when to play. There is a rhythm to life that makes it work. Nature's rhythm gives us the cycles of life. By understanding how everything in life moves in cycles, we become more aware of and comfortable with our own cyclic nature.

Almost every culture recognizes the presence of cycles, and this awareness is represented in circular art, calendars, and astronomy. In Greece, Pythagoras proposed a cyclical model of the heavens. The Mayans developed a calendar based on the rhythmic cycles of energies. The goddess Kali in India demonstrates cycles of destruction that are required in order for something new to be created. The mythical phoenix, a bird that burns itself to ashes in order to be reborn, illustrates the cyclical nature of life. Artistic representations of cyclic rhythms have been dated as far back as 4500 BCE on Chinese vases showing self-devouring serpent designs. The ouroboros, the circular snake that eats itself, is an ancient mystical image that shows that the end of anything is also the beginning. The symbol of a coiled snake represents the cyclic properties of the universe. In fact, the snake has been seen as a universal symbol of reincarnation for at least six thousand years. Other cyclical designs have been found in Babylonia, Iran, India, and Egypt.

Ancient people understood that time was cyclical. Early Greek philosophers proposed a cyclical movement of the stars; in the book of Ecclesiastes, the Bible refers to cycles, stating that for everything there is a season and a time for every purpose under the sun. In his personal journal, on August 23, 1853, Henry David Thoreau expressed appreciation for all of nature's cycles, advising us to: "Live in each season as it passes; breathe the air, drink the drink, taste the fruit, and resign yourself to the influences of each. Let them be your only diet drink and botanical medicines. . . . Be blown on by all the winds. Open all your pores and bathe in all the tides of Nature, in all her streams and oceans, at all seasons."[1]

LINEAR TIME: A MODERN CONSTRUCT

Modern society no longer sees time as cyclic. We typically view time as linear, stretching from the past into the future, with one sequential event following another. Why is this significant? Because the way we understand time has a tremendous effect on our thought processes. The modern view of time gives us a preoccupation with progress, and devalues periods of rest that are a necessary part of the cycle.

Even our seasons reflect that the timing of nature is cyclical, not linear. Spring and summer bring growth and progress, while autumn and winter are the part of time's cycle that slows us down or brings us rest. Because we no longer value time in a way that allows periods of rest as well as times for productivity, we have changed our viewpoint of what is natural. Such thinking has led humanity to try to control nature, rather than recognizing that humans are part of nature and, as such, we need to live within its rhythms. An example of this arrogance is the blatant cutting down of trees, either to procure lumber for building or to make roadways through the rainforest. Trees provide a necessary balance between oxygen and carbon dioxide in our air. When we ignore or dismiss the importance of this cycle of gaseous exchange provided by trees, we destroy the very air we breathe.

Rather than accepting the inevitability of cycles in life, patriarchal cultures encourage learning from past mistakes and moving forward. But history never actually repeats itself exactly. Each moment has a different energy, and we ourselves are different in each moment. Therefore, learning from history only reinforces the mistakes we previously made, keeping us locked into old beliefs and old patterns of behavior when we should be responding to the new creative energy of the present moment. There is no freedom to feel the energy that is present now and respond accordingly if we are focused on a past that has already happened or a future that has not yet arrived.

Unlike the Western, linear view of reality, Earth-based cultures model their behavior on observations made about nature, which moves in cycles of change. They observe that life consists of interconnected processes rather than separate occurrences that progress linearly. Nothing exists exclusively by itself. African, East Indian, Chinese, Native American, and Aboriginal cultures all believe that, like the things they see around them in nature, reality is also cyclical. The connection between health, growth, and honoring natural cycles is clear. Honoring all natural cycles helps us to deeply grasp the understanding of just how nonlinear nature is, and therefore how nonlinear life is. The crescent moon always becomes full and then becomes crescent again. The death of tree leaves fertilizes the ground for new seeds to grow. Events in nature are not directional in a linear sense, but are always circular and connected.

Earth-based cultures recognize that life cycles into death and back into life again, in an unbreakable pattern of interconnection. In India this idea is understood as reincarnation. It is believed that one's choices in this life bring repercussions in the next life. The effects of our actions in one life accumulate, creating karma that must be resolved in the next cycle of life through making better choices. Time, through which these cycles can be seen, is a process, not a series of events.

ALL OF LIFE IS RHYTHMIC

Life is rhythmic. The rising and setting of both the sun and the moon cycle in rhythm. The ocean's tides, seasons of the year, and even the stock market function in cyclical rhythmicity. Periodic behavior is especially obvious when one examines any aspect of time. More than twenty-three hundred years ago, Aristotle noted cyclical swelling of the ovaries of sea urchins at the full moon. Haemophilus of Alexandria recorded daily cycles of pulse rates. Cicero wrote that the flesh of oysters waxed and waned with the moon. In 1954, Romanian historian of religion, fiction writer, philosopher, and professor Mircea Eliade proclaimed in *The Myth of the Eternal Return* that the reappearance of cyclical theories in contemporary thought was pregnant with meaning, stating: "Just as the disappearance of the moon is never final, since it is necessarily followed by a new moon, the disappearance of man is not final either; in particular, even the disappearance of an entire humanity (deluge, flood, submersion of a continent, and so on) is never total, for a new humanity is born from a pair of survivors.

This cyclical conception of the disappearance and reappearance of humanity is also preserved in the historical cultures."[2] Others have also asserted that since so many biological rhythms have been discovered, it is simpler to assume that everything is rhythmic unless proven otherwise. Life on Earth is defined by cyclical processes.

The understanding that living organisms cyclically flow through ecosystems is one of the basic concepts of ecology. Each ecosystem is marked by exchanges of energy and resources and everything that happens therein is connected to a universal system. Communities of organisms have evolved in ecosystems over billions of years, continually using and recycling the same molecules of minerals, water, and air. Physics explains that matter and energy transform from one to the other and then back again in a continual process. The biological cycle of plants, for instance, consists of solar energy transformed into chemical energy by photosynthesis. The late visionary dancer Emilie Conrad and the renowned neuroscientist and pharmacologist Candace Pert assert that physical processes are not things; they are activities that take place in an open, fluid system.[3]

Life on Earth is defined by cyclical processes that reflect duality. These processes can be seen as cycles of creation and destruction and are absolutely necessary for life to exist. They are characterized by the process of photosynthesis, which is the building of plants through the use of carbon and their disintegration in decomposition. Volcanoes eject huge amounts of carbon dioxide and plants recycle this carbon dioxide into oxygen through photosynthesis, keeping the atmosphere balanced in order to sustain life. As part of an ecological system, volcanoes, hurricanes, and other so-called destructive forces are necessary in order for life on Earth to continue.

Chaos theory shows that greater and greater complexity causes movement toward a bifurcation point, where transformation can occur. This point is a place of infinite possibilities that cycle around a strange attractor called change. In the midst of this complexity, stable cycles suddenly return. Catalytic cycles are at the core of self-organizing chemical clocks of life. The lava that spews forth from a volcano in time becomes the fertile soil for plants to grow; the riverbed that overflows brings minerals to enrich the soil; from the enriched soil, life springs forth anew and balance is maintained.

The lives of whales, swallows, butterflies, and even rocks are marked by cycles. Layers seen in rock patterns demonstrate cyclic patterns of water and rock movement. Rocks have been in motion for millions of years, shaping and reshaping the face of the Earth. Plants and animals do not live apart from these movements; their own life cycles are immensely influenced by the cycles of Earth's movements. Movement of the Pacific tectonic plates consumes rocks, for example, creating bays and deep-sea canyons. Plants and animals are born, die, and eventually turn back into rocks. Life cycles from plant to rock and back again, re-creating itself in different forms as the environment changes. Movement is implicit in nature's cycles because motion promotes change.

CIRCADIAN RHYTHMS AND OTHER HUMAN CYCLES

Circadian rhythms (defined as inner cycles connected to the Earth's cyclic periods of day and night) abound in nature. In protozoa and algae there are twenty-four-hour periods regulating photosynthesis, cell division, movement, and luminescence. Plants possess diurnal rhythms governing the movement of leaves and the opening and closing of flowers. Some animals (whales and swallows) migrate in a cycle consisting of a series of seasonal return migrations between feeding ranges and breeding ranges. Twice a year, the entire population of Pacific grey whales swims to and from their summer feeding grounds in the Bering Sea. Some insects (the butterfly) begin cycles that are completed by their offspring.

Humans, as part of nature, are also governed by circadian rhythms. These rhythms are important for human health, safety, performance, and productivity. The circadian clock not only regulates our twenty-four-hour rhythms, but is also involved in the regulation of rhythms of much longer duration, such as women's monthly hormonal changes and seasonal sleep changes. Seasonal changes in night length induce parallel changes in the duration of melatonin secretion, with the result being that the human sleep cycle is longer in winter and shorter in summer. These changes in duration of nocturnal melatonin secretion, in turn, trigger seasonal changes in behavior. Behavioral changes paralleling cyclical seasonal changes can be seen in both animals and in humans.

Every part of being human includes a cycle of some sort. More than one hundred functions and structural elements in humans oscillate between maximal and minimal values once a day, including our breath, our blood, and our hormones. Every day our bodies produce more than 300 billion new cells. We take more than seventeen thousand breaths and average thirty thousand blinks of the eyes every day. Our hearts beat more than two-and-a-half billion times in an average lifetime. It is difficult to find any aspect of being human that does not include some kind of cycle. However, humans have done their best to ignore natural cycles, abandoning natural human rhythms for the more controlled industrial, technological rhythms of life. As previously discussed, the technological acceleration of rhythms in day-to-day living is an affront to the human nervous system and contributes to our separation from nature and from each other. What we choose to eat and drink also contributes to this unconscious imbalance we help to create in our lives.

Every parent is proud when her child learns to talk or walk, indicating progress toward growing into adulthood. Yet this same progression ultimately leads to death, and unless death is considered part of the life cycle, its arrival can make our progress seem meaningless. When seen as part of nature's cycles, death is perhaps the ultimate act of renewal!

Humans must recognize the natural cyclical processes of life and death, for excessive reliance on linear thought or a cultural orientation toward progress alone is disharmonious with the natural world. Moving away from the natural order of life seems to move the individual closer to disease. Renowned attorney and legal advisor Julian Gresser shared the term *hurry sickness* with me in a personal conversation. It describes the relentless progress that takes us away from the natural, sacred cycles of the seasons, the winds and the tides, and most directly, the rhythm of our own human bodies.

FOR OPTIMAL HEALTH, WE NEED TO HONOR OUR CYCLICAL RHYTHMS

In disease etiology and treatment, physicians recognize the importance of some biological cycles, although most physicians are painfully ignorant about the importance of honoring our most basic hormonal cycles. Western physicians take advantage of the rhythmic regulation of cell division in the treatment of cancer, and they recognize the importance of some natural cycles such as the need for regular sleep and proper nutrition. Yet other cycles are completely ignored.

Through a more systemic approach, Eastern medicine gives greater importance to the recognition of all the different cycles that affect health. For example, recurrent weather conditions such as winter cold can reactivate dormant health problems including arthritis pain; summer heat can affect the heart. Cyclic processes are at the foundation of the theory and practice of Chinese medicine and its older East Indian sister, Ayurveda. In the Chinese five element theory, each of the elements (representing a specific organ in the body) is related to an element preceding it and one following it. Too much or too little of one element causes the next element to be out of balance as well. As each organ is affected, the one next to it is affected, completing a cycle of health or disease.

Ayurvedic medicine defines energy systems as chakras that govern the movement within certain areas of the body. When a person is healthy, each chakra systematically moves in harmony with the other chakras. When energy in one of the chakras becomes stuck, the person loses their harmonic balance. Ayurvedic physicians also incorporate an understanding of seasonal cycles in diagnosing illness and prescribing remedies. Specific characteristics aligned with seasonal attributes are considered because, according to Ayurveda, health is only achieved by honoring the process of movement between seasons, conditions, and choices.

Immune, endocrine, hormonal, and nervous system cycles are part of vital information processing that makes a total functioning system in humans. To achieve health, we need to move away from perspectives of causality that focus on separate issues and move toward a deeper investigation of and respect for the information gained from examining all cyclical systems and the wisdom and harmony they provide. The use of pharmaceuticals can have a cascading effect of deteriorating health because such treatments focus on singular issues rather than on the entire system. In contrast, bioidentical hormones compounded to match our cyclical nature communicate through a nonlinear process of information exchange: cycles.

Although cycles are evident throughout the universe, it's curious that one of the most obvious cycles on Earth (women's monthly bleeding) is often minimalized, controlled, or even ignored in the West, as are natural hormonal cycles in men. Ignoring these cycles, or trying to control or suppress them (as with birth control pills), is an act that removes us from nature and from the balance that is inherent in cycling as part of life. We become out of balance when we argue with or ignore Mother Nature.

THE IMPORTANCE
OF BREATHING CORRECTLY

Breathing is also a cyclical process. A great similarity exists between women's cycles and breathing cycles. Exhalation and inhalation are both necessary to sustain life. Likewise, it is necessary for women to experience both the letting go and the building up of blood within their bodies to create life. Both cyclical processes are acts of renewal. Discharging old blood and discharging used air are both necessary. Blood renews the possibility of creating life, and breath renews the energy of the body to sustain life. Breathing cycles and blood cycles both have merit in showing the relevance of honoring the timing and versatility of nature. If one cannot breathe out strongly and thoroughly enough to allow a proper inhale, the breathing cycle cannot function optimally. The essential exchange between carbon dioxide and oxygen is thus thwarted, and life becomes a struggle from the deepest core of existence: our breath.

Ukrainian scientist Konstantin Pavlovich Buteyko believes that carbon dioxide is the master hormone of life because it regulates all activity. If our breath does not flow in and out naturally, we stress the entire system. Indeed, shallow breathing is endemic to our overly technological lifestyles. Technologically driven humans are literally not running on all cylinders. Because they are disconnected from their own life rhythms, they lack depth. Often they cannot relate to others because they are disengaged from their own natures. You may notice that such people are frequently addicted to and continually use caffeine, sugar, or other artificial stimulants to recharge their already overly burdened systems.

Because all systems are connected within the body, when we struggle to breathe, our immune systems are compromised through the stress. This understanding illustrates how deeply we are connected to the basic cycling of life within our bodies, that of the carbon dioxide–oxygen exchange. How many doctors understand this primal hormonal activity and monitor the entire system by examining our cycles of breath?

At this point, stop and notice how *you* are breathing. Notice how others around you are breathing. How many of us take time to breathe fully and properly when we are caught in the urgency of pushing ourselves forward to the next task? If we listen closely, can we hear the spaces where we are holding our breath, waiting for something or afraid of something? Can we notice how often we inhale but forget to consciously exhale?

Most people do not even know how to give (or receive) a proper hug, one that allows at least one full cycle of breathing to connect to the other person (an interesting observation brought to me by my wonderful partner, Cullen, whose insights into human behavior are deeper than those of anyone I know). The linear focus of living in progressive societies and the lack of honoring our natural human cycles increase our tendencies to grasp at everything and hold on to it, even our breath. We do not really know how to let go of what needs to be released in order to allow space for the next opportunity or the next breath to arrive. The fact that women in modern cultures try to push through days when they are releasing blood as if they were ordinary days shows the severity of the problem. We are culturally unable to let go, to slow down, and to rest. Is it any wonder that the highest values in modern societies produce competition, greed, and fear?

SOCIAL CYCLES AND NATURAL CYCLES

Our relations with others also reflect whether we are in balance or not. We are social beings, constantly interacting with others—whether through intimate partnership or with children, family, neighbors, work, or even total strangers. In relationships, attachment and separation are part of the cycle of human life. It is easy to see cycles in infancy and childhood when, as children, we make increasingly broader discoveries about ourselves and the world. Each new realization brings the child back to a new place of questioning within the cycle. Cycles are also easy to see in adolescents as the search for the balance between identity and intimacy appears.

Adult cyclical interactions are not always as obvious as children's cyclical interactions are. Most people cycle in and out of the need to be alone and the need for companionship. Healthy relationships recognize that cycles occur as part of the relationship, like everything else in nature, and they honor the importance of each part of the cycle. A good relationship is a process of continual change as it reflects new issues, deals with challenges that arise, and uses the resources available in each situation. Unfortunately, in our modern societies, the natural, healthy cycles within relationships are often disregarded because our media has romanticized intimate relationships so much that often people discard their partners the minute the fairy tale seems to stop. Instead, it would be prudent to work through the cycles of highs and lows that intimate relationships offer as a way of growth.

Cycles map the most auspicious time for everything in life. Women are fortunate enough to have an internal map that gives them directions for the most auspicious timing for everything they do. Unfortunately, our Western culture has decided that women's inner guidance system is relatively obsolete, and has reprogrammed women to abandon their internal twenty-eight-day biological calendar in favor of a patriarchal calendar. Indeed, in our modern societies, it often may seem inconvenient to follow Mother Nature's directives. Many of us may wonder how we will get everything done if we stop or even slow down. But if we don't allow the exhale and rest period during the release part of our natural cycles, we find ourselves exhausted. If we insist on continually being active, we're robbed of the energy necessary for our creativity. This type of pressure is perilous, instructing women, as it does, to conform their cycles of rest and creativity to a patriarchal five-day-on, two-day-off artificial cycle.

The following are some small steps we can take every day to slow down the frenetic pace of our lives: set limits on how often you check your email; cut your to-do list in half and relegate the second half to the following week; identify the people or situations that drain you and resolve to reduce your interactions with them if possible.

Devaluing natural biological rhythms harms men, too, although the timing may not be as clear. Men's cycles are governed by regular hormonal changes that may also occur in rhythm with the moon.

However, the rise and fall of testosterone is not as marked as a woman's menstrual cycle. Be this as it may, men are affected by major shifts in the balance between testosterone and estrogen ratios in their hormonal makeup as they age. We need to begin to pay attention to the biological rhythms that cause change within each of us, women and men alike.

BENEFITS AND BALANCE DERIVED FROM THE MENSTRUAL CYCLE

The portion of a woman's cycle that pulls us more into ourselves in order to cleanse what we no longer need and to change what is not working is usually viewed as a time of general disgruntlement, where legitimate complaints women may experience are labeled as a simple result of where the woman is in her cycle. Emotions are often discounted as merely being a manifestation of premenstrual syndrome (PMS), rather than being valued for what they might actually express about a woman's life. Premenstrual syndrome is a clinical medical diagnosis, however, our culture has adopted the policy of ascribing all cyclical changes in women to PMS, assigning culturally negative values to what are inherently positive attributes.

Ignoring a woman's cyclical nature isolates her from processes that occur as a matter of course, the knowledge of which may very well bring balance and benefits. Detachment from bodily changes can lead to repression of the benefits of those changes. With a loss of connection to one of nature's most powerful rhythms, women may lose the sense of balance within themselves, their relationships, and their world. I see evidence of such imbalances every day when women stop in the middle of a doorway, oblivious that someone else wishes to pass, or make sudden lane changes without warning when they are driving. Or they simply change their minds quite frequently, without regard for how these changes may impact others. Such impulsive changes cause many women to be viewed as unreliable whereas men who fail to honor the flow of natural cycles are deemed to merely be inflexible. Balanced human beings are able to navigate cyclical changes with both flexibility and reliability. Culturally, we seem to have lost that ability, and it is going to take a deeper awareness of the presence of the cyclical nature of the divine feminine within all of us to reinstate a harmonious balance once again.

The moon rules the flow of fluids (both ocean tides and individual body fluids), including the timing of the menstrual cycle, the fertility cycle, and birthing labor. These cycles, specific to women, offer an opportunity to truly understand the magnificence of being part of the natural world. If we are not in tune with our own rhythms, then we experience sharp and inappropriate breaks or alterations in living rather than experiencing life as a cyclical and steadily unfolding pattern.

Thus as women, we also experience duality in that we have the natural opportunity to experience life as it presents itself to us externally—and internally, when it presents as inward movement within us. As creatures who experience such a personal sense of duality, the waxing and waning cyclical processes guide us. Even the planet Venus, a physical representation of the divine feminine, presents two faces on Earth (morning star and evening star) depending upon where the planet is in the sky during different times of the year (a cycle in itself). Perhaps these varied positions of Venus are a reflection of the ability of the divine feminine to see from more than one perspective—something all of us would be wise to incorporate into our lives.

If we ignore, control, or deny the importance of our own cycles and the gifts of women's dual nature, we are likely to experience far-reaching effects that are unpleasant in nature. We are seeing some of those unpleasant repercussions today: an increase in stress, a lack of connection within relationships, a greater frequency of illness, the deepening of frustration and sadness, the rise of clinical depression, and a decrease in creativity on all levels (including, broadly speaking, infertility and intuition). Our evolution as a species is being thwarted by imbalanced patriarchal concepts. We can no longer allow the essence of who we are to be hidden under patriarchal dominance. Through an expanding appreciation for the divine feminine and an understanding of all cycles, women and men can learn a great deal about how to live with respect for each other and for all of life; we are all part of nature!

2
Biology and Healing

THE CURRENCY of patriarchal culture is progress, and progress assumes continual advancement. Retreat, the opposite of advancement, is often considered failure. By this standard, women, who have a natural biological urge to retreat once a month, are considered failures in our culture if they choose to honor a time of retreat. Therefore, women are encouraged to be the same every day to meet the standards of the patriarchy. Reliability means constancy in modern cultures.

CONSTANCY IS NOT NORMAL

Expecting each day in a woman's monthly cycle to be the same is artificial and unrealistic. Failure to perceive a woman's need to respond to life differently during different times of the month isolates women from a biological process that occurs anyway, causing confusion and imbalance. Being in harmony with the process rather than detaching from the bodily changes that occur leads to an increased wisdom about one's very own nature.

As a psychologist observing the general population, I have seen that women are often too slow or too quick to respond to changing circumstances, which indicates a long-term imbalance within cycles. Consider your own observations of yourself and others. Are you someone who stops in the middle of a supermarket aisle deciding what article to purchase without noticing that you are blocking others? Do you suddenly change your mind when you are driving and change lanes without warning, endangering others? Do you constantly and inappropriately vary your speed when driving? Do you find yourself overreacting to some circumstance because the natural outlet for your feelings has been suppressed for far too long? I am not by any means suggesting that women are inferior. However, long-term disregard for one's cyclical nature can lead to confusion about how to operate in the daily world. A continual push for constancy, progress, and control is fundamentally responsible for damaging our ability to listen and respond to our own inner guidance, which is biologically designed to help both men and women participate in life more easily and more naturally.

The imbalanced patterns I observe in men, influenced by attitudinal choices and hormonal imbalances, manifest as an increased need to control, exemplified by impatience, aggression, and intensified expressions of anger. Very simply, we are all out of harmony with nature, as evidenced by our behaviors, our choices, and our lifestyles. It is possible that continually living in such an imbalanced state will eventually lead to our extinction.

The divine feminine presence is urging us to listen to our hearts and return to a participation with nature, rather than trying to control her. A good place to begin is through reexamining our viewpoints and misunderstandings about women's cycles and how they can support the return to a balanced way of life for all of us. Environmental cues such as light, the effect of ocean tides, and the movement and phases of the moon all play a role in regulating women's menstrual cycles and fertility.

Like the moon, women go through a period of darkness each month. Most women begin their menstrual periods during the dark of the moon, starting to bleed between 4:00 a.m. and 6:00 a.m. Although we accept the inevitability of the phases of the moon, natural phases experienced by women are not accepted for their many benefits, even when evidence points to a strong link between the moon's influence on the Earth and on the natural cycles of women.

HORMONES AND HOW THEY FUNCTION

To understand the differences experienced by women throughout their cycles, which helps us understand cycles of all humans, we must understand how hormones operate. A hormone is a product of a living cell that circulates in body fluids and produces a specific effect on the activity of cells remote from its point of origin. In *Listening to Your Hormones,* women's health educator Gillian Ford defines hormones as chemical messengers sent out by the endocrine glands, which control or stimulate hundreds of vital processes and act on almost every cell in the body.[1] In *Screaming to Be Heard,* E. L. Vliet, M.D., refers to hormones as chemical communicators that carry messages to and from all organs of the body.[2] In *Women's Moods,* Deborah Sichel, M.D., and Jeanne Watson Driscoll, Ph.D, PMHCNS-BC, describe the fertility cycle as the result of an intricate, precise dialogue between brain and ovaries.[3] The fertility cycle presents a picture of the constantly changing hormonal environment.

Hormones influence our growth and development, mental alertness, and sleep patterns. They affect every aspect of our being, and yet we are ignorant of the role our hormones play in determining who we are and how we behave. How many people realize that vitamin D is an essential hormone and not a vitamin? How many people know that two primary hormones, insulin and leptin, influence all other hormones and regulate our body's rhythmic activities? Leptin controls the thyroid, regulates our sleep, orchestrates our inflammatory response, and decides whether to make us hungry or to store more fat in our bodies. Together, leptin, insulin, and vitamin D are key to our survival, affecting our emotions and our behaviors. Yet, most of us are ignorant about the hormones that cause us to function normally in homeostasis.

Because we are out of harmony with nature, we continually make choices that further deregulate our hormonal systems. Irregular sleep patterns (undermining the production of leptin), unhealthy food choices and skipped meals (affecting our progesterone), and staying inside all day (affecting our vitamin D levels) rather than walking in the sunshine as our ancestors did, cause further hormonal imbalance. When these underlying hormones are seriously imbalanced, our endocrine system destabilizes, beginning with the thyroid, the master gland that regulates other glandular activities. We do not need to study the medical science of hormonal and endocrine systems to understand how to come back into balance. We simply need to follow the call of the divine feminine and return to living in harmony with nature. Understanding women's cycles is a great starting point to lead all of us back into rhythmic harmony.

Hormone receptors are more prevalent in certain areas of the body, including the limbic area of the brain (which controls emotions), the adrenals, the breasts, the ovaries, the uterus, the testicles, and the digestive system. These hormone receptors transmit information to a cell's DNA, allowing important chemical changes to occur. When hormone levels are low, their receptors decline in number. The estrogen receptors increase and decrease depending on the phase of the menstrual cycle in women; a decrease of testosterone in men occurs as their estrogen receptors increase.

THE MENSTRUAL CYCLE AND ITS PHASES

Menses occurs on average every twenty-eight days, counting the first day of flow as day one in the fertility cycle. Medically, women's cycles can be divided into the luteal phase, from ovulation until the onset of menstruation, and the follicular phase, between menses and the next ovulation. During the luteal phase, growth and development of an egg occur biologically, and the prepared egg is propelled into the fallopian tube. Progesterone is almost absent at this time, during which the endometrial lining in the uterus gradually builds up, preparing to receive and nourish the egg in the event that pregnancy occurs. Just before mid-cycle, estrogen levels drop precipitously, and luteinizing hormone (LH) is released in a mid-cycle surge that causes ovulation. Ovulation brings an abrupt rise in the neuropeptides of follicle-stimulating hormone (FSH) and LH. If physical conception does not occur, the uterus lining is expelled in menstruation, and the cycle continues into the luteal phase again.

More than forty recent scientific studies show the magnitude of changes during the menstrual cycle, including temperature and hormonal changes, dream cycles, behavioral changes, and mood differences.[4] A woman's temperature cycles diurnally; it is consistently lower at night than day, and seasonally is lower in October and November than in May in the northern hemisphere (lower in April and May than in November in the southern hemisphere). This pattern appears regardless of ambient external temperatures. Women prefer a higher room temperature during the luteal phase of the menstrual cycle than during the follicular phase, and in the morning as compared to the evening. Additionally, there are both quantitative and qualitative differences in the circadian levels of peripheral blood immune cells during different states of a woman's cycle. Tryptophan metabolites are elevated during both the luteal and premenstrual phases compared to the follicular phase of women's cycles. L-tryptophan is a precursor of serotonin. The interaction of gonadal hormones with the serotonergic systems likely contributes significantly to behavior and mood changes during the menstrual cycle. Such strong biological markers indicate a very real and necessary acknowledgement of the unique ways women experience the world.

Numerous studies show that women perform at a higher level in tests of articulation, mental arithmetic, manual speed skills such as finger tapping, and simple repetitive tasks during the follicular phase of their cycles. Plasma estrogen levels are also elevated at the ovulatory phase. Furthermore, specific aspects of memory may also covary with plasma sex steroid levels across the menstrual cycle.

My own studies found a statistically significant increase in creativity during the follicular phase of women who allowed themselves secluded, quiet, and introspective time during the menstrual phase of the cycle. Additionally, women show differences in their dreams according to their monthly cycles, with increased REM periods, a greater requirement for sleep, and a sense of feeling better if they sleep longer during the premenstrual phases of their fertility cycles. Likewise, sexual content of dreams changes with hormonal changes of the fertility cycle. In my research, I found a statistically significant increase in the number and meaning of dreams in women who secluded themselves in a sacred space during menstruation. There appears to be a relationship between the level of estrogen in a woman's body and her degree of dreaming, as well as her memory of her dreams.

Many hormones cycle through the human body (female and male) on a daily basis, in accordance with circadian rhythms. Additionally, many hormones act as neurotransmitters in all humans, demonstrated particularly by the presence of FSH and LH in women. Both women and men produce the hormones testosterone and progesterone. Testosterone levels cycle daily; these levels are highest in the morning, upon awakening, falling by as much as one-third to one-half throughout the day. It may surprise some people to know that sexual experiences stimulate a rise in testosterone in women more than it does in men. For both genders, general testosterone levels rise with experiences of success and fall with experiences of failure.

The hormones estrogen and progesterone affect nerve cell functions. Estrogen produces progesterone receptors and primes them to work. Progesterone, produced by the adrenal glands and increased when we are under stress, can switch the estrogen receptors either on or off. These events are constantly happening, back and forth, on and off. Thus, it makes sense that hormones have profound influences in behavior, mood, and the processing of sensory information during the menstrual cycle. Men are affected by hormonal cycles, too. Precipitous drops in progesterone levels can lead to angry moods, aggressive behavior, and disrupted sleep. Understanding that hormones influence how we (both women and men) interact in the world, could be profoundly important in accepting our place as part of nature.

THE MASK OF NORMALCY THAT WOMEN WEAR

Many women indicate that they feel more positive mood states in the follicular (ovulatory) phase than they do in the luteal (menstrual) phase of their cycles. The luteal phase, from ovulation until the onset of menstruation, is the time women are most in tune with what is not working in their lives. By denying the importance of different perceptions that arise during various phases of a cycle, women remove themselves from their natural ability to flow with nature and make necessary changes, thereby limiting accessibility to their own inner wisdom and power. The wisdom contained within a woman's body is a most potent wisdom. If we deny what we know intrinsically, we disempower ourselves from sharing our wisdom with others, allowing the world to continue on a path that can disenchant or dishearten us.

Are women supposed to always be pleasant and smiling? Or can women be allowed to honor the darker emotions that demonstrate that something is wrong in their relationships, their homes, and/or in the world? I am not willing to adopt the medical viewpoint that women should simply accept a diagnosis of hormonal imbalance when they visit the dark side periodically in order to see what needs clearing out and changing. Women are biologically designed to slow down, go inward, look at their lives, and assess the changes that need to occur once a month. If women do not consciously take this path, then emotions that are expressed unconsciously are often labeled hysterical or pathological. Culturally, we are completely remiss if we simply accept labels such as PMS that mask symptoms of imbalance. Perhaps now more than ever before, our struggling world has a great need for tears of angst and anger that stimulate change.

Many women see their natural biology as something that is wrong and needs to be corrected, controlled, or medicated to be healthy and whole. Indeed, the study of women's cycles has become big business in recent years. The traditional medical model of examining women's cycles does so from the position of diagnosing individual symptoms rather than looking at the whole picture, causing the prescription of far too many inappropriate pharmaceuticals and labeling imbalances as syndromes. Traditional medicine even prescribes birth control pills to regulate when and how much women bleed. If attempts are made to artificially control the fertility cycle, pathological problems frequently manifest. Oral contraceptives have been shown to eliminate part of women's hormonal communication pathways, including sexual communication with men. Specifically, women taking birth control pills do not secrete the volatile fatty acids in vaginal secretions (known as copulins) that stimulate male sexual interest and behavior.

Why are there so many misunderstood aspects of the menstrual cycle, in spite of clear biological evidence that should make comprehension of it relatively simple? Obviously, the linear scientific approach to studying women's cycles is not the best approach. Modern society would benefit from holding a more holistic view of both women and men, as part of a more holistic view of all of nature. Again, if women's cycles are taken apart and their various component parts studied individually, whether that be hormones, behavior, or mood differences, there will always be a lack of complete understanding of the whole picture. Coupled with the cultural directive to treat every day the same (systematic homogenization), any attempt to control women's bleeding illustrates a total disregard and lack of understanding of the gifts of having a dualistic cycle. Progressive thinkers including the medical doctors Christiane Northrup and Michael Platt argue against the male dominator model of medicine, which has misinterpreted and controlled the role of the female menstrual process for far too long.

A CLOSER LOOK AT PMS

The patriarchal need to control nature and the lack of attunement to the natural biology of women causes stress, which immediately disrupts hormonal balance and often results in a woman having to seek medical attention. The diagnosis of premenstrual syndrome (PMS) is one possible outcome of experiencing natural changes in one's body in a culture that requires constancy in mood and behavior.

While premenstrual syndrome was originally defined as a hormonal imbalance infrequently occurring in severe conditions, our current conditioning leads us to accept its apparently increasing prevalence as a natural part of being a woman. As a result, monthly changes that occur as natural and normal differences are now often viewed as pathological. The *Diagnostic and Statistical Manual of Mental Disorders* lists specific symptoms of depressed mood, tense or anxious mood, frequent tearfulness, persistent irritability or anger, decreased interest in usual activities that may be associated with withdrawal from social relationships, difficulty concentrating, feeling fatigued, marked changes in appetite, insomnia, breast tenderness, headaches, bloating, and a sense of being out of control under the disease category premenstrual syndrome. These symptoms occur in a cyclic pattern, beginning before menses and ceasing abruptly once bleeding has begun. The traditional medical community has accepted the umbrella diagnosis, and unfortunately, many women now believe that any of these symptoms are treatable offenses and seek pharmacological help to alleviate them regardless of the trauma such treatment causes the physical and emotional bodies. Western society views women as victims of their hormones. Sadly, many women accept the label of PMS as a convenient way to dismiss the truth that something in their lives needs to change. Traditional medical practitioners have been slow to follow the lead of alternative champions like doctors Michael Platt and Christiane Northrup in dealing with this issue.

Premenstrual syndrome is a phenomenon that does not exist in indigenous cultures. Earth-based cultures understand and appreciate the fact that when a woman is in the process of cleaning out what is no longer needed (uterine lining and old problems), the veil between everyday understanding and special, intuitive understanding is very thin. It is extremely unfortunate that such a delicate connection has been so maligned and labeled as a syndrome, and that the accompanying emotions signaling need for change are dismissed as only an outward sign of a hormonal shift. A woman's tears during her sacred cycle are much more closely related to the salt tide of the ocean and they may erupt in order to point out that something needs to change. We have no business trying to rationalize emotions away by stating that they are largely the result of hormonal activity. Hormones are messengers, directing our attention to both natural shifts as they occur in the body, and imbalanced places in our psyche that need our attention.

ADDITIONAL FACTORS
LEADING TO IMBALANCE

Women today are also subject to becoming unbalanced by the ingestion of animal hormones in food, toxins in the air and water, too hurried a pace, and society's demands to be what we are not. Men are equally affected by the toxins in our environment, eating foods laced with animal hormones, and an unnatural pace of continual and hurried progress. Is it any wonder that we are seeing more depression and anxiety, and more addictions of all kinds—both overt and hidden—in both women and men? Is it any wonder that overall, our culture exhibits more anger, more violence, and more feelings of being out of control than ever before?

I once volunteered my skills as a psychologist for women in jail. In only a few years, the number of women in that jail increased from five inmates to sixty. I offered volunteer counseling sessions for some of these distraught women who were angry at losing their sense of belonging in the world and were, in my estimation, totally bereft of wisdom about who they really were. They had lost a sense of balance within themselves, and this imbalance was reflected in the choices and actions that had landed them in jail. Although I did not work with the male prison population, I suspect the loss of harmony with nature has also caused an increase in men's choices and actions, with the end result being that they too end up in jail. Our modern competitive culture leads both genders into aggressive and defensive behaviors that cause harm to themselves and others. There is a complete and total lack of awareness of how to achieve the highest good for all through harmony and cooperation.

In addition to witnessing the anger in the female prison population, I see evidence of repressed anger in the clients that I treat therapeutically on a daily basis. I see it in the behavior of the general population when I am moving through my life. Unaddressed, unresolved anger can surface as inappropriate road rage or manifest as some other form of physical, psychological, or emotional violence. Both women and men are frightened of rage that is out of control, and rightly so, for this anger may become explosive. Such behavior is disconcerting to everyone, both the person experiencing the emotions and those individuals who are on the receiving end of them.

This kind of displaced anger destroys relationships and eventually destroys the self, leaving cinders of regret and waves of guilt in its wake. The woman who is angry every month and doesn't understand why, or the man who reacts unpredictably in anger, does not know how to use anger for positive change. It is time that we examine causes of such imbalances rather than simply labeling them.

Our bodies, female and male alike, which are largely made of water, respond to the gravitational pull of the changing tides of our planet. Our muscles, largely made up of water, and our brains, primarily made up of water, are susceptible to such gravitational forces. How can ignoring such prodigious differences in human cycles in any way honor the naturalness of who we are fundamentally, either as women or men? A number of studies report a significant difference in the levels of mental distress women experience according to where they are in their fertility cycles. As far as I know, science has not studied cyclical patterns of mental distress in men. Yet both women and men are often medicated with mood-elevating drugs rather than examining what is not working in their lives. If depression is only treated with pharmaceuticals rather than examining its underlying causes, it only takes one further away from living an authentic life as one's true self.

We all experience distress if our feelings are ignored or if we are continually told that our problems are medical only. There is absolutely no place in our culture for accepting unhappiness as a necessary part of a cycle that's designed to create productive change in one's life. Cyclical emotional releases in both genders are signposts pointing the way to change if we open our eyes and look at them.

Honoring emotional signals as they naturally occur does not, however, mean that we are entitled to use our emotions to manipulate others or to unleash those emotions—including blame and judgment—in a way that causes harm to others. The modern-day psychological perspective that we have a right to our feelings has sadly promoted an associated belief that we also have the right to release our feelings on others, without taking responsibility for those feelings. Again, our emotions exist to show us what is out of balance so that we can make changes. They were never intended to be used as tools for manipulation, control, judgment, or blame. When we spend quiet, private time with our own emotions, we can find the wisdom to guide us on how to act to make necessary changes in our lives.

CONTRIBUTING FACTORS:
A FEAR OF DEATH AND A REVVED UP LIFESTYLE

When examining this lack of acceptance of natural cycles in our culture, I would speculate that the lack of acceptance of women's natural cycles could be partially related to a larger fear—the fear of death. We are able to accept that leaves fall from trees, decay, and new leaves come again in the spring. Yet death connected with blood appalls us, and we turn away from women's blood as if it will contaminate us with the scent of death by its very presence. But death is a reality, just like a woman's monthly menstrual cycle is a reality.

Women have the greatest understanding of the connection to life and death in the blood of their bodies. One of women's key roles in life is to share the importance of cycles and thereby steer us all away from uniformity and inappropriate consistency. We live in a political climate that spews dogma about respecting diversity, yet the diversity women bring at a biological level remains completely disregarded. We must allow and support the cycles that promote positive change in our lives. We must allow death to come to the emotions, beliefs, and situations that are no longer appropriate to us in order to create more harmonious and cooperative living as well as a greater sense of our own well-being.

Because women are no longer openly setting the example of cycling as part of nature, humans have abandoned natural human rhythms and adopted artificial rhythms of life. These artificial rhythms include disregarding circadian rhythms to work or play on the computer at night, or not resting during menstruation, for instance. Women in particular suffer, struggling to survive in an environment that demands they continually adapt their natural rhythms to an artificial schedule. I see that many, many women have become imbalanced as a result of this behavior, causing them to be confused and uncertain in decision making, something that does not happen nearly so often when women honor their natural rhythms.

Additionally, we have not only disregarded natural rhythms, we have accelerated the speed of life, adapting ever more quickly to technological innovations and discoveries, making us increasingly hard wired to expect constant changes. These changes adversely affect our nervous systems. Additionally, the effects of these changes are reflected in mounting numbers of physical and emotional maladies, including the number of children who are diagnosed with autism, attention deficit disorder (ADD), and/or attention deficit hyperactivity disorder

(ADHD). Perhaps these children are simply too sensitive to cope with the rate of incoming information that assaults them on a daily basis. Increased depression, anxiety, and anger, increased heart disease and obesity, increased autoimmune problems, are all results of ignoring nature's pleas to return to a state of balance. The late world-renowned dancer and visionary Emilie Conrad often said that we are allowing a mechanistic way of living to endanger our lives as bio-humans; in short, our love affair with machines at the cost of valuing our natural rhythms is pulling us toward our own extinction.[5]

Women's cycles can act as a primer for all of us to understand the various aspects of who we are. How we relate to women as they change each month can teach more respect for nature in all her changing forms. It's obvious when looking at the seasons of the year that nature decrees a right time for everything. As humans, we may participate in that timing; we may pick berries in the summer and read by the fire in the snowy winter. Yet often we fail to participate in the natural timing of our own cycles. If we can understand and respect how endemic cycles are to all of life, perhaps we can increasingly interact with nature as participants rather than as controllers of it. Such interaction brings healing, directed by inner wisdom, from cycles of change.

3

Religion Replaces Spirituality

WHEN I WAS A TEN-YEAR-OLD steeped in the Christian doctrine of my tribe, I asked the preacher of my church a few puzzling questions. I was having trouble understanding exactly how a woman was made out of a man's rib. It did not make sense to me that man was made first, and then woman was formed from a portion of his body. Given that, in my young experience, girls seemed to catch on to things quite a bit faster than boys did, and girls were definitely better at getting good marks in school, sometimes ran faster, and seemed more interested in making things (while boys tore them apart) . . . why, exactly, was it that we were made *second?*

Perhaps there was an error in the preacher's lesson that women came second to be a companion for man. I thought perhaps the Creator really had made man first as a practice run and then refined the creation on the second go-round. I also did not understand why the church was teaching me that I should not listen to my body; that it would betray me or lead me astray. So far, when my tummy said I was hungry, I was. And when I stubbed my toe and felt the pain, I knew to pay attention. So in what way was my body going to betray me? Little did I know that the coming fertility cycles signaling sexual maturity threatened the church that fed me these spiritual tenets.

Later, while I was being coached through a Southern girlhood with advice such as, "Let the boy think he is smarter than you," I decided that there was something seriously flawed with that system. Why couldn't I just be myself?

THE MAKING OF A SECOND-CLASS CITIZEN

Matters didn't get much easier. At the age of twenty-two, I was castigated for being an old maid because I was not yet married and later, when I finally did marry, I lost my excellent credit rating to my husband (who, incidentally had no credit until he married me), simply because he was considered to be the head of the house. I was outraged that I was the one who was working, paying all the bills, balancing the household accounts, and my credit record (so carefully built as a single woman) was suddenly taken from me and assigned to him, an unemployed young man in school!

My questions about the order of things and, particularly, my place as a female in society, such as it was, caused me nothing but trouble until I moved from the South and the politics of the times caught up to my own beliefs about the way things should work. How had we arrived at a position of having to hide part of who we are as women? At what point did we move from accepting our nature to hiding in shame? How did men become the accepted leaders and the ones who made all the family (and/or community) decisions? The answers to these questions lie in the evolution of humans from hunter-gatherer societies to agricultural societies, and with that change, the movement from nature-based spirituality to a patriarchal religion.

In her book, *Rebalancing the World,* scholar and educator Carol Lee Flinders explains that hunter-gathering people upheld these values of belonging:

▲ Connection with land
▲ Empathic relationship to animals

▲ Self-restraint

▲ Conservatism

▲ Deliberateness

▲ Balance

▲ Expressiveness

▲ Generosity

▲ Egalitarianism

▲ Mutuality

▲ Affinity for alternative modes of knowing

▲ Playfulness

▲ Inclusiveness

▲ Nonviolent conflict resolution

▲ Spirituality[1]

These qualities were valued by both genders in hunter-gatherer societies. The arrival of agriculture rearranged the way people lived, causing a shift in values. The new patriarchal system had new goals, and therefore new values that conflicted with the old ways of living. The old values were cooperative; the new values were competitive. Rather than discarding the old values altogether, however, they were shifted into the domain of women, who continued to live by them.

Even so, the men quickly discarded the old values of cooperation for the competitive values that Flinders identifies as the new values of enterprise (listed below). It soon became apparent that the values upheld by women were in direct conflict with the new patriarchal values. The newly forming patriarchy grew strong, the values of that system became entrenched in the people, and they were passed down as the values by which we live today:

▼ Control and ownership of land

▼ Control and ownership of animals

▼ Extravagance and exploitation

▼ Change

▾ Recklessness and speed

▾ Momentum and high risk

▾ Secretiveness

▾ Acquisitiveness

▾ Hierarchy

▾ Competitiveness

▾ Rationality

▾ Businesslike sobriety

▾ Exclusiveness

▾ Aggressiveness and violence

▾ Materialism[2]

I would put separation at the top of that list. Drunk with the pleasures of ownership and control, humans began to move away from the land and their relationship to the land as nature beings. With the exception of indigenous cultures, which were incredulous that someone could even think of owning our Mother Earth, our ancestors gave up the nomadic, land-based way of living and adopted a more settled lifestyle. They made a stark move away from being children of the land to being landowners.

The switch from spiritual connection with the land to dominion over it bred concepts of competition and acquisitiveness. Humans, who had always shared everything with generosity as indigenous cultures still do today, changed value systems with one swift discovery that being in control brought power. Under the tutelage of men, women were taught that control also brought safety and comfort, so it became more palatable and pervasive.

THE ILLUSORY CONSTRUCT OF CONTROL

Being in control is addictive; it offers a strong sense of safety. However, by contrast it suggests that a lack of control means uncertainty. The effects of this belief system have grown and impacted our freedom. We can see an example of how this works by looking at what happened when the Twin Towers in New York were attacked on September 11, 2001. After that occurrence, the United States government created the Department of Homeland Security, feeding its citizens the old patriarchal creed that additional control would keep people safe.

Such ideas about safety, however, are an illusion. The catch is that in the hunter-gatherer societies and Earth-based cultures, uncertainty and lack of control were managed through a spiritual understanding of life cycles and the idea that Mother Earth could and would provide for all living things. Everything cycled, so therefore a cycle of provision would surely follow a cycle of need. Today we have lost our trust in natural cycles and replaced that lost trust with an ever-growing sense of fear, allowing the illusion that more and more control can keep us safe.

These shifts in beliefs began with the coming of agriculture, when indigenous beliefs and values were pushed aside or assigned to the realm of women, as humans moved from equally valuing the connection of all things to a position of dominance over the land. Mother Earth was no longer treated as a living being supporting humans and animals and plants. To humans, She became inert land to be controlled. The first agriculturists decided which plants were crops and which were weeds and began to exert control over their placement and their growth. Rivers were dammed or diverted to control their flow. Rather than belonging to the land, agriculturists claimed ownership and dominion over it.

The arrival of Christianity supported the rising belief that dominion was superior to belonging, and a doctrine was born to support a new myth that man was given dominion over the land and all her creatures. With such a powerful shift from land-based spirituality to the written word of an abstract god, people lost the holiness of being part of nature and the importance of listening to bodily awareness. The body was cast out as a detractor; something that interfered with the higher mind and the progress of humanity. This shift in belief killed any ideas of gender equality. Women, life-givers who had enjoyed full awareness of nature's cycles through their own bodies and who used the wisdom from those cycles to guide their communities, lost the ability to keep the balance through their innate understanding of the creative gifts of their dual natures.

On a planet where duality infuses everything, the loss of understanding of such a gift created enormous imbalance, for women have always taught by example how to honor the cycles of life and death through their inner understanding of duality. As people began to claim the land rather than continue to move in nomadic patterns, women no longer worked side by side with men as partners. The labor was divided into roles that were increasingly gender specific, and men became more responsible for the decisions that were made outside the home. Women were now largely relegated to producing sons and caring for the now permanent home. They had lost their power, their self-confidence, and their self-esteem.

Values of belonging are indistinguishable from worldwide Earth-based values, which are based on cooperation. Despite the power shift detailed above, in virtually all Earth-based cultures, women enjoyed equal status with men, and in some of these cultures, they were even in charge. Women, and the cycles of life that are part of their nature, were honored in traditional indigenous cultures because women are uniquely able to bring life into the world. The new patriarchal Christian culture did its best to eliminate rhythms of life in order to instill sameness (being stuck, lack of creativity, and control). The rules of the new church were strict and unaltered by circumstance. Being in rhythm with nature became an affront to God.

THE FURTHER DEMOTION OF WOMEN

In the new system women were no longer seen as productive when they slowed down to honor their natural biological rhythms. Even withdrawal from normal duties because of pregnancy or childbirth now allowed more control of external affairs by men, who through new eyes were beginning to evaluate everything in terms of progress. Slowly women lost their ability to participate in decisions that affected them and their communities. The intuitive wisdom of women that came through their dual nature and their times of bleeding were no longer honored or respected. Their insights and ideas were no longer sought; in fact, intuition quickly became something that was feared by men and hidden by women; women were even labeled witches for knowing things intuitively. Men who exhibited the intuition of the divine feminine were equally condemned.

As this trend continued, intuition became a secondary value ascribed only to women, a lesser thing to be discounted in the wake of increasing scientific facts. The strength required for childbearing was turned into a time of frailty, and the pain of childbirth was viewed as a punishment for women's leading men away from their god. When the new myth proclaimed that Eve caused both she and Adam to be cast from the Garden of Eden for eating from the Tree of Knowledge, beliefs were set in place to devalue any knowledge a woman might contribute that was derived from the divine place of intuitive wisdom. The truth is that intuition is an aspect of the divine feminine and is equally present in both women and men.

Current Christian mythology does not mention Adam's first wife, Lilith, a strong and independent woman who was equal to her husband. Lilith refused to be controlled by a man, and choosing freedom over submission to another, she left him. Christianity erased Lilith from the myth because her feminine strength equaled Adam's masculine strength. The new mythology assigned her to the wilds of the subconscious that needed to be controlled, if she is addressed at all. She became the temptress, eager to lead men astray.

A new wife for Adam, Eve, was created for the new mythology. Some theories say that Lilith became the snake who offered Eve the apple, encouraging her to claim her divine right to knowledge, thus supporting the view of Lilith as a temptress who led people away from God.

According to the new Christian myth, because Eve had been formed from the rib of Adam, she could never be whole; she would always be only a shadow or a part of a whole person. This view led to the common belief that married partners complete each other, rather than honoring the truth that each person is whole and complete within himself or herself. The erroneous belief that we as individuals are made complete by our partners is reflected in our language today, wherein men and women refer to their spouses as my other half or (worse) my better half. The Christian Church devised a philosophy called original sin in the new mythology, which gave Eve the responsibility for the fall of man from the Garden of Eden.

This belief system has shaped the idea that women are being punished by monthly bleeding (often called the curse, as we know) and pain from childbirth for tempting men to engage in the fruits of the mundane world. It is more likely that the new way of living that denied natural rhythms created stress, causing hormonal imbalances that led to pain and cramping with monthly bleeding, and more difficult and painful births. Modern medicine attests to the fact that constant stress causes a continual flow of adrenaline while the person (female or male) continually tries to survive while living out of harmony with nature's cycles of rest and activity. Excess adrenaline cascades into other hormonal imbalances that have been reflected in physical imbalances and emotional extremes in both women and men.

While gifts of the divine feminine were increasingly undervalued and discounted, even the gift of bringing children into the world became a duty to be performed for the landowner husband. Every landowner needed sons to strengthen his legacy of ownership and control over increasingly larger domains. Rather than nursing and caretaking each child for an appropriate amount of time, women were encouraged to produce more sons more quickly in order to carry the family acquisitions forward into the next generation. Slowly even women's power to bring forth life became another event under the patriarchal control.

As time progressed after centuries of dominance, the divine feminine refused to be suppressed any longer, spurring political movements for equality; the Women's Liberation Movement was born. Women gathered together to restore their place beside men. However, in the desperate cry for equality, the pendulum swung too far in the other direction, resulting in a struggle to prove that women could be more like men, rather than arguing the benefit of feminine duality. Women began to hide their monthly cycles of bleeding so they wouldn't be viewed as inferior. Years of negative beliefs about menses fostered the view that menstruation was something debilitating, inconvenient, and undesirable, something that removed a woman from society's demand for constant progress. Unless a woman was trying to conceive a child, menstrual cycles were viewed simply as an inconvenience to be ignored, a nuisance in the way of more socially acceptable things, such as bringing home more money, building careers, or gaining political office.

THE FURTHER MANIPULATION OF WOMEN'S NATURAL CYCLES

The importance of cycles of life as revealed through women's duality was almost completely lost with the advent of birth control pills. Suddenly millions of women consented to (or even asked for) the regulation of their natural cycles for the sake of convenience, ignoring the natural beauty and relevance of their own rhythms. One result of this artificiality was to force all women taking birth control pills into an often unnatural twenty-eight-day cycle, a severe step that completely disregards individuality. With this huge shift of priorities, women forgot their inborn understanding of the importance of their own natural timing and the art of going inward when nature called. This artificial tampering severed or badly injured women's remaining connections with intuitive guidance, which was already devalued in both women and men. The loss of right timing and intuitive guidance, accompanied by the dismissal of women's thoughts and feelings as unimportant, led to deeper frustration, grief, and further hormonal imbalances for women and a greater sense of separation from men.

It was in this milieu that premenstrual syndrome was born. PMS, which has become a household word in Western societies, was brought forth from the cries of hundreds of thousands of Western wombs that were suffering from an artificial scheduling of sacred cycles and a general lack of regard for women and gifts of the divine feminine. Although there is a place in medical classification of disease for extreme hormonal imbalance that requires outside intervention (diagnosed as premenstrual syndrome), the PMS that most women believe they experience could be simply the subtle announcement of moving into another way of being during natural cycles of change. The hormonal shifts women undergo every month just prior to the arrival of the time of flow have physical attributes such as tender breasts, water retention, and occasional headaches. There are accompanying emotional changes in the form of increased emotional sensitivity and awareness of disharmony. Neither of these categories of change are pathological; they are merely signals to women (and men) that it is time for women to slow down, withdraw, and honor the process of change within.

Because political structures are so intricately intertwined with religious beliefs, the change from spiritual values to religious values deeply affects the selection of governmental leaders. Values that uphold competition and control are not in alignment with values that utilize quiet periods of personal contemplation in order to achieve more cooperation in the world. In my lifetime I have heard outrageous arguments that women should be disqualified from corporate roles or major political offices (such as president) because possible PMS reactions could trigger war!

Men fear the emotional changes that actually serve to guide a woman in making important decisions. However, no one addresses the increasing emotional extremes experienced by men in leadership roles, as they and society become more and more imbalanced through cultural devaluation of principles of the divine feminine. In fact, it appears that men have become more emotionally unpredictable as humanity has stepped further away from natural rhythms and respect for natural life cycles. As the patriarchy increasingly tries to control nature and the divine feminine, the consequences become exceedingly more dire.

Fortunately, there is a movement (of both men and women) advocating a return to the principles of the divine feminine. Women are finally achieving political posts and positions of importance in corporate America, but usually such a success occurs because a woman has aligned herself with the prevailing patriarchal values and disconnected herself from any cyclical wisdom. Not choosing the right person for an important position because of gender-based assumptions that women are more emotional than men is a tragic mistake, one that simultaneously dismisses the wisdom of emotional guidance in women and ignores emotional reactions in men.

A NEED FOR NEW CULTURAL CONSTRUCTS

The different ways that we treat public displays of emotion in women and men comes from the values upheld in our cultural myths. If we want to change the imbalances between the way women and men are treated, we need new stories, new myths, to uphold new values. One of our most familiar cultural myths has shaped the treatment of women by teaching that Eve sinned (made an error) by discovering forbidden fruits (knowledge) offered to her by the intuitive wisdom arising from the Earth Mother (the snake). Actually, the knowledge she discovered was body knowledge, a way to experience heaven through connection with another human: sexual connection. Eve, through the tutelage of the snake (possibly Lilith), discovered how to move from duality into oneness. In other words, Eve followed her natural instincts, discovered the delight of unity with man, and was condemned for knowing that she had the power to bring forth life.

With the advent of agriculture, a nature-based spirituality of respect and connection could not support the emerging value system of competition and aggression. A new story was needed to uphold the new values. When hunter-gatherers began to settle into permanent communities, Mother Earth, spiritual progenitor for all life (and hence, female, since only females can bring forth life) was pushed aside for a new king—a divine male image that was wrathful and all knowing. The divine feminine was thrust, literally, underground. The snake, which through its ability to shed its skin had heretofore represented the ability to shed what was not needed and go inward to find wisdom, came to represent evil.

Patriarchal cultures fear snakes and what they represent: the ability to shed what is irrelevant in life, to go underground for wisdom, and to bring forth new answers. Snakes and women have both been feared and dismissed in the current cultural myths. Since the snake has been relegated to tempter (or temptress) rather than wise guide in the Judeo-Christian creation myth, many people today have a deeply instilled phobic reaction to both snakes and menstruating women. This viewpoint evolved from the construction of a myth that placed men in the role of givers of life: a male deity and a male rib formed the first woman. The idea of a woman's connection to life and death through blood was also changed to support the belief that it was men, not women, who were important. The ancient icon of the mother pelican piercing her own breast so that her drops of blood would feed her nest of newborn chicks was usurped by Christianity and replaced by the sacrificial bleeding heart of Christ.

THE LARGER ROLE
OF RELIGION IN ALL OF THIS

In 2009, former President Jimmy Carter made a powerful public statement about the unequal treatment of women that arose through church misinterpretations of spiritual tenets. Part of his public statement, first published as an op-ed in *The Observer* on July 12, 2009, is printed here.

> I have been a practicing Christian all my life and a deacon and Bible teacher for many years. My faith is a source of strength and comfort to me, as religious beliefs are to hundreds of millions of people around the world. So my decision to sever my ties with the Southern Baptist Convention, after six decades, was painful and difficult. It was, however, an unavoidable decision when the convention's leaders, quoting a few carefully selected Bible verses and claiming that Eve was created second to Adam and was responsible for original sin, ordained that women must be "subservient" to their husbands and prohibited from serving as deacons, pastors or chaplains in the military service.
>
> This view that women are somehow inferior to men is not restricted to one religion or belief. Women are prevented from playing a full and equal role in many faiths. Nor, tragically, does its influence stop at the walls of the church, mosque, synagogue, or temple. This discrimination, unjustifiably attributed to a Higher Authority, has provided a reason or excuse for the deprivation of women's equal rights across the world for centuries.[3]

In the Christian Church today, the sacrament is taken in the form of red wine as a symbol of the blood of Christ. But red wine had been used as a symbol of the blood of the Great Mother, the Holy Woman, for centuries before Christ. In many cultures, ceremonies took place in which women and men would take the symbolic blood of life in the form of red wine—for example, in the Dionysian mysteries and in tantric rituals. Sometimes this partaking of wine was acknowledged as a symbol of menstrual blood, the magical fluid out of which human life was created. Blood has always been the main symbol for the wellspring of existence and the mystery that sends us forth into this life. The fact that women bled once a month meant that they were closer to this wellspring.

The Judeo-Christian religion fosters a view of women as lacking in spiritual values and being unclean, lesser beings, particularly so when they are menstruating. Even today Orthodox Jewish men refuse to shake hands with a woman because she may be menstruating. This mindset reversed the reverence for the divine feminine, declaring men were the ones more closely connected to God, or the Divine.

This viewpoint is extremely contrary to indigenous views that a menstruating woman is so powerful that she could change the shape of the world! To create life, to bring a child into the world, is the most powerful thing in Creation. A man's power is nothing compared to this.[4] A wise man would respect that power, because unlike the myths that define women as weak during their menstrual flow, women actually are particularly strong at this time.

In any event, the shift from divine feminine spirituality to patriarchal religions of control placed men in the place of the Creator, or most closely connected to the Creator. Women were assigned less important roles, given that they had simply been taken from the rib of a man, according to the new myth. The power and divinity of the process of birth was devalued and became a duty; sacred cycles were considered a punishment. And the divine feminine was marginalized and then eclipsed.

Removing women from the position of divine life-givers required debasing the treatment of women's cycles as well. Part of the problem is that the start of the fertility cycle announces that a woman is a sexual being, which suggests creative power. Having the power to create also suggests having the power to destroy. Recognition of this dangerous and dual power caused a fear in the men who wished to be in control, and subsequently, a disempowerment of women in the Christian Church. Religious dogma replaced the peace, balance, and harmony of nature-based spirituality.

Christianity is not the only religion whose patriarchal, dogmatic values have reduced women to subservient positions. In verse 33:53 of the Qur'an, Muhammad gives instructions to men about interactions with women: "Whenever you ask them for anything that you need, ask them from behind a screen. This will deepen the purity of your hearts and theirs." The Prophet's instruction was to drop a curtain (not a veil) between male strangers visiting his home and the women they addressed.

This instruction was meant to enhance respect for women by protecting them from men's lustful looks, but it was twisted after the Prophet's death. Reversal in the social status of women began by requiring them to wear veils outside of their own homes. Fundamentalist ideologies have overridden the wise view of Islamic leaders such as Mohammad Ali Jinnah (the founder of Pakistan). Pakistani activist and the youngest-ever Nobel Prize laureate, Malala Yousafzai, quotes him in her book *I Am Malala,* saying, "No struggle can ever succeed without women participating side by side with men. There are two powers in the world; one is the sword and the other is the pen. . . . There is a third power stronger than both, that of women."[5]

Perhaps we now have a better understanding of how women have been alternately viewed as dangerous, less capable, or more delicate than men. Or perhaps this viewpoint is too scary, too threatening to examine deeply by those who are comfortable with the existing paradigm. However, anyone with an iota of conscious awareness can see that our world is out of balance and the elements of cooperation and harmony are missing at almost every level. Predominant religious systems based on patriarchal beliefs support a creation myth that continues to place men in control and women in subservient positions. Far too often women are portrayed as being less valuable than men, or equally disturbing, as sexual temptresses who lure men away from the cherished beliefs and values of the patriarchy.

In *The Dream of the Cosmos,* one of the most profoundly important books of our time, author, lecturer, and Jungian analyst Anne Baring writes:

The two great religious meta-narratives in Western civilization—the Myth of the Fall and the Doctrine of Original Sin—created a dualistic belief system that split nature from spirit, and body from mind and soul. They taught generations of men and women that this world was a place of suffering, sin and punishment, and that the spiritual life demanded a rejection of this world, [creating] a pathology which is deeply embedded in a religion that is now embraced by over 2 billion people. It constitutes an unconscious collective thought form which is extremely difficult to transform and heal because it is so deeply unconscious.[6]

As I look back at my ten-year-old questions and sense of the world, I understand the confusion I experienced. Of course I tried to live by the values of my tribe, and in the process I learned to deny that what my body told me was true. Now, as a postmenopausal woman, I reflect on the fact that because of cultural persuasion, I denied or ignored the gifts of women's cycles for a large part of my adult life. I fervently wish to prevent other women from making the mistake of detaching from or being embarrassed by their dual natures. And I wish to help men understand how to awaken to the gifts of the divine feminine that live inside of them, just waiting to guide us back into harmony.

Personal growth is not necessarily a linear progression of increasing speed, and duality is necessary for us to be able to see and understand the whole from different perspectives. Slowing down, looking and listening deeply to nature, and sharing with others frequently solve more problems by creating a harmonious lifestyle than our hurried, progress-oriented modern pace. Quiet, intuition, and cooperation are divine feminine values worthy of being recaptured and practiced. The duality of women and their accompanying cycles must be viewed not merely from a biological perspective but from an understanding of the feminine connection to divine cycles of all of life and a guiding force for all of humanity.

4

Blood Mysteries

⚭

SOME YEARS AGO I stood in the Stanford Research Park at Stanford University in California, staring at the enormous statues carved by the men of Papua New Guinea: huge penises and men with wombs; penises with a bowl beneath them and carved figures of gods emerging. As I stood in the midst of the statues, creation myth stories poured out of the art like the blood they depicted. In Papua New Guinea, it is believed that while women can give birth to children through their blood, men give birth to the gods through male blood. Since men do not have a monthly bleeding cycle, male kings ritually slit the underside of their penis and drip blood into a bowl, ceremonially giving birth to the gods. They see this act as the secret of Creation, for without this ritual, the world would no longer exist. Staring at the statues, I was in awe of the depiction of the jealous longing of men, a longing so strong it had produced a male facsimile of women's monthly bleeding.

Reaching further back into history, we find that when men understood that women were able to create new human life through the power of their blood, Mayan men, like the New Guinea men, decided that they could create the birth of gods by shedding their own blood in a similar ceremony. The king was thought to have the most potent blood among humans; therefore, he was the focus of tremendous power.

His intentional taking of his own blood was thought to bring the gods to life and divine power into the lives of the Maya.

Throughout history, blood has been deemed to be an integral component of the processes of life and death. Whether blood is produced through wounding or flows naturally as it does during menstruation, every culture in the world gives special meaning to the flow of blood. Most people have strong beliefs about blood; beliefs that have been passed along through stories that may be the same for women and men or that may differ. Each civilization passes down these stories, or myths, about life and death, about blood, and about the balance of power between men and women.

Today most people are confused about blood. Many Westerners seem to be captivated by its presence, as evidenced by the abundance of horror movies and video games that are part and parcel of our culture. Others are indifferent to the presence of blood and removed from its meaning, as evidenced by the countless deaths depicted on television, video games, and movies. Whatever the cultural position, blood stands for life, thus the shedding of blood can be frightening, dangerous, and/ or mysterious.

Below we will explore some cultural and historical perspectives about blood, about menstruation, and how beliefs about blood have influenced the balance of power between women and men. It's an interesting narrative, no matter its cultural spin. We'll start by looking at male and female views of blood; then we will investigate a few myths about blood and power that will provide a deeper understanding of the balance between life and death.

WOMEN'S AND MEN'S VIEWS OF BLOOD

Women and men have different views of blood. Typically, men think of blood as being connected to injury or death, a symbol of something being wrong. In modern cultures, women also have been taught to view blood as an indication of something gone awry, and thus they often feel inferior whenever they themselves bleed. Yet it is a fairly recent state of affairs for women to believe that something is amiss whenever they discharge lifeblood. In fact, if you ask most modern Western women to address their views of blood, they'll speak of blood with revulsion, as in blood produced from injury, violence, or war, or as a nuisance, as in the blood of their own monthly cycles. Often it seems they would like to ignore blood completely. While the aversion to blood from injury or death has not changed much historically, modern views about menstrual blood are very different from the views of our ancient sisters!

In most cultures women's menstrual blood is considered to be very different from blood that comes from injury or death, although the connection is clearly apparent—from blood new life springs forth. Shedding blood indicates death, whether it is an actual death resulting from wounding, or preparation for a child that is not to be created. Women have a special perception about the meaning and cost of shedding blood; they understand at a bodily level the vulnerability of human flesh. How easily it can bleed! The natural processes of menstruation, childbirth, and menopause initiate women into deep understanding, perhaps in a way that a man can never conceive (pun intended).

In most Earth-based cultures women are aware of the effect of the gravitational pull of the moon on them and on their blood. Women can feel the internal pull of the tides in their own bodies, whether they heed this rhythm or not. Women feel fuller and emptier at certain times of the month. Because women's adult bodies, which are approximately 60 percent water, routinely release and replenish their blood, they notice the gravitational pull of the moon more than a man does, just as creatures swimming in the ocean feel the ocean tides more than land-based creatures do.

Historically men have been warriors and hunters who have seen the loss of blood as a step toward death. Usually they were the ones to initiate the bleeding, either through warfare or the hunt. Men's views of blood throughout history have also been linked to power. Male views of menstruation, accordingly, reflect the loss of blood as a step away from life. Islamic men consider menstruation to be a wound. According to the Qur'an, even though bleeding during the fertility cycle is natural, it upsets people's sense of what is whole. Verse 222 states that menstruation "Is a harm, so keep away from wives during menstruation." This view of women's bleeding indicates that a woman may be vulnerable during this time, which elicits a tender concern for women. However, in both Jewish and Islamic traditions, modern interpretations (by men) have often been translated to insinuate that menstruating women are impure or dirty, even though the Qur'an clearly specifies that women are not prohibited from any type of spiritual worship during menstruation.

Further, modern Islamic men have expanded on the importance of women's blood by making it a cultural requirement for a newly married woman to have a nonelastic hymen that produces blood upon the first instance of sexual penetration by her husband. The importance of the hymen's capacity to bleed profusely makes it the most essential part of a girl's body because it supposedly proves her virginity. Some women may be injured and lose their hymen through no fault of their own, or some women may even have a congenital absence of the hymen. Because in Islamic culture women's blood is somehow connected to honor, these women suffer a terrible cost for being different.

In the Egyptian culture, blood is also connected with honor, and a new bride is expected to bleed from the puncturing of her hymen. A new husband pays the bride's mother for maintaining her daughter's honor with thirty rials in cash and the bloodstained handkerchief he produces after the wedding night. However, because all honorable unmarried women are assumed to have unbroken hymens, gynecological examination of virgins is rare. Genetic anomalies in the lack of a hymen or prior injuries are never taken into consideration. Punishment for a lack of blood on the wedding night is harsh and can lead to the girl's being killed by her family for being dishonorable. Clearly this gap in understanding the female body is costing some of our sisters dearly, even today.

Male beliefs about the fertility cycle have varied culturally through time, yet it is generally agreed that men have traditionally viewed menstrual blood with awe or fear. The fact that women could produce blood monthly and not be wounded caused reverence in some cultures and fear in others. The late Emilie Conrad explained that in ancient phallic societies, women had tremendous power.[1] Because men associated women's mysterious bleeding and capability of creating life with power, they feared the loss of their own influence in their cultures. As they sought more influence for themselves, they began to dismiss women's contributions as being unimportant or irrelevant. Again, disempowering women became a way for men to gain control.

In cultures that feared menses, menstrual blood was considered to have power. The Gimi of Papua New Guinea saw menstruation as a constant threat to male purity and superiority because menstruating women were deemed to be very powerful. Although some tribal men believed blood could be powerful enough to bring death, most North American tribal men approached menses in a spiritual way, as a power that could bring good or evil. Men accommodated women's bleeding for the welfare of their women, their community, and their country. When the women requested sacred spaces for retreat while they bled, the men built houses for them to honor their request for separation during this powerful time.

Many African tribal men also shared this approach to menstruation. The Beng in Africa believe that menstrual blood is special because it carries in it a living being. An analogy here would be that of a tree: before bearing fruit, a tree must first bear flowers. Menstrual blood is like the flower that must emerge before the fruit—the baby—can be born. A spiritual approach to women's bleeding honors and allows women to have a greater sense of their own power and unique attributes.

Anthropologists have argued that the sight or thought of a person who bleeds from the genitals (a menstruating woman) could be frightening to a man, who naturally protects his protruding genitals and, as part of his protection ideology, carries an intense castration anxiety. Others have embraced the view that men were generally frightened by any loss of blood and reacted by trying to avoid it. Yet while avoiding blood, men were envious of women's capacity to bleed from the genitals without being wounded, and blood initiation rituals to emulate women's blood-making and childbearing powers were born from this envy.

Many modern-day men view the bleeding cycle with a mix of awe, fear, and/or revulsion. According to the Hindu Laws of Manu, if a man even approaches a menstruating woman he will lose his wisdom, energy, sight, strength, and vitality (a clear recognition of women's power, although reflected in fear-based beliefs). Traditional Chinese have a similar reaction to menstruating women, since they think of all bodily discharges as unclean and dirty, although they also think of it as being powerful because it is a life-giving substance. Menstrual blood is extremely potent because it is inherently powerful as a necessary precursor to the creation of life. However, because a menstruating woman is temporarily the bearer of a powerful and potentially harmful substance, Chinese men and women see the presence of menstrual blood as disturbing to the gods.

Respect and reverence for the ability of women to bleed without injury as a natural phenomena have been replaced by analytical examination of chemical hormonal changes or ignorance and confusion surrounding this most precious of times. Many men today are left believing that menstruation is indeed a curse that causes great confusion, emotionality, and unnecessary unpredictability in women.

MENSTRUAL BLOOD'S LINK
TO POWER ACROSS CULTURES

The blood of menstruation has been referred to as sacred or supernatural in many ancient cultures and most if not all of these societies came to believe that all blood held power, particularly menstrual blood. In most ancient cultures, the power of blood was neither bad nor good, but it was perceived to be dangerous because of the change it could bring.

Indigenous people understood that change in some form always accompanied the presence of blood. Change was not necessarily harmful, but it could be if not treated properly. Cherokee women take measures to seclude themselves during menstruation and childbirth because both events involve blood and are considered to be associated with a spiritual power that is so strong it can overwhelm medicine, spoil crops, or incapacitate warriors. Consequently, men respect these potential dangers and keep their distance. This voluntary seclusion of the women is one way they signify their power, for the intricacies of the rites they perform in private to control and channel their own power is known only to them. In Australian Aboriginal cultures menstrual blood is also sacred and powerful. Here, too, men avoid menstruating women so this sacred fluid specific to women will not overpower them.

Like the Cherokee, Yurok women secluded themselves during their flow because it was believed that a woman was at the height of her powers when she was bleeding. The Diné (Navajo) also referred to menstruation as a time when women have their power. Around the age of ten Diné girls were prepared for the power they would possess. They were taught by elder women how to avoid harming others. The Diné believed dangers from menstrual blood increased with age. By contrast, the Anishinabek believed menstrual blood was more powerful in a woman's first cycle. According to them, first blood held so much power that it was possible for plants to die if touched by a woman menstruating for the first time, and fish could die if she entered a lake or stream. Because of this, an Anishinabek woman would not even look at anyone except female elders during this time, for her glance could cause an unintentional aim of power that could create tension or cause harm.

Lakota women also took protective precautions by isolating themselves and not interacting with the rest of the family during menstruation. Native American poet, novelist, and critic Paula Gunn Allen summarized in *The Sacred Hoop: Recovering the Feminine in American Indian Traditions:* "Women who are at the peak of their fecundity are believed to possess power that throws male power totally out of kilter.

They emit such force that, in their presence, any male-owned or [male]-dominated ritual or sacred object cannot do its usual task."[2]

Menstruating women were considered to be in the midst of their own powerful ceremony, a ceremony of life, so they avoided other ceremonies during menses. A Hopi woman told anthropologist Ruth Underhill in 1930, "We have power. Men have to dream to get power from the spirits and they think of everything they can—songs and speeches and marching around, hoping that the spirits will notice them and give them some power. But we have power . . . children. Can any warrior make a child, no matter how brave and wonderful he is? Don't you see that without us, there would be no men? Why should we envy the men? We made the men."[3]

Other cultures believe that it is the responsibility of bleeding women to learn how to channel their power for the good of the community. Older women teach younger women, who first begin bleeding, the importance of directing their inner power in order to prevent unpredictable changes that may affect anything or anyone in the community. If the women of a culture have lost the understanding of this skill or fail to teach it to their young women, menstruating women are avoided.

In Portugal even today a menstruating woman is often avoided because it is believed that her powers for change could cause plants to wilt or objects to move inexplicably. Menstruating women who have little or no control over their special powers can bring chaos to their physical environment simply by their presence. The Kalahari Kung of Africa believe that a menstruating girl has great supernatural powers that can be harnessed for the good of the community if rightly respected. Believing that the power of blood is able to provide for their needs, they use the blood of a menstruating girl to bring luck to important occasions. Celtic myth holds the belief that any drop of falling blood, whether male or female, is dangerous and has corrosive powers that can cause infirmity. The Celts also believed that only if blood were mixed with the energy of love could its corrosive powers be neutralized.

In Europe and in colonial America, women's menstrual power was so feared by men that they created a mythology of witches, producing a legacy of dishonoring and persecuting women. When the patriarchy took over, puritanical beliefs prohibited discussion of the fertility cycle or other bodily functions, and the sacred power inherent in women's wisdom came to be feared rather than respected. Cast into the role of witches, women who had knowingly avoided attending community fires during their bleeding cycles now found themselves burned at the stake in these same fires. This example points to how the power of menstrual blood has often been misunderstood in Western cultures, which filters these views through Christian myths about childbearing and sin.

LIFE OR DEATH? SEEKING BALANCE

Sixteenth-century Pueblo Indians believed that the world was made by throwing a clot of blood into space, thereby bringing power into the Earth. The Diné (Navajo) believe the first fertility cycle is a symbol of the restoration of power and fertility on Earth and a cause for great rejoicing. The Acoma Indians believe that plant and human seeds alike hold the potential to generate life. Seeds planted in Mother Earth or a child planted in its mother's womb repeats the cycle of life. All indigenous people held a clear recognition of the need for balance, both between life and death, and between genders.

The necessity of balancing the power between men and women is reflected in Earth-based cultures worldwide. The wise women of the female shamanic line of the Sami people in Sweden still work to maintain practices for balancing power between genders and with the Earth. But much of that understanding has been lost in modern societies because so many indigenous people have had to adapt to the white majority's cultural myths and religious beliefs in order to survive. Only in patriarchal societies do women struggle to maintain their own power so that the balance between genders is equitable.

In Native American societies, women may segregate themselves on certain occasions, but on other occasions men are also segregated. Every ritual depends on a balance of power. It is understood in indigenous cultures that a woman's power and a man's power are opposites, like hot and cold or day and night. Men's power is typically more related to fire and women's to water. During menstruation the balance between the masculine fire and the feminine water is shifted because the amount of water carried by women increases. During this time the increased water in a woman makes her stronger. It is believed that this increase of feminine water-energy can quench a man's fire, so it is best for both men and women that these energies not be mixed during this time.

The presence of blood reminds us of the connection between birth and death in the human life cycle. Blood flows out of the body (or dries up) at death. Blood is the fluid that ushers in a new life at birth. In the earliest human cultures, birth was deemed to be a magical act; the magic of birth was a complete mystery. Later cultures noticed a connection between birth and women's cycles of bleeding. In Greece, Pliny the Elder called menstrual blood the material substance of generation. Maori myth says that human souls are made of menstrual blood. African myths speak of the congealing of menstrual blood to make humans. South American Indians believe all people are made of moon blood. The Aboriginals consider salt water, which comes from the womb of the sea and has the taste of blood, to be regenerative in the same way that the blood of a pregnant woman brings life to a child. Seawater is known to be healing and regenerative for all who need to bring new energy into their lives. Respect for the ocean's regenerative powers is even linked to modern superstition—fear of spilling salt is directly related to the idea of spilling blood.

Aboriginal people believe that death and initiation are the same thing. The blood of birth is inseparable from the blood of menstruation or the blood that can accompany death. Because of the difficulty of separating them, all occasions of bloodshed, whether through menstruation, birth, or death, are considered dangerous, and the need for balancing those forces is paramount. Life and death, blood and power, balance and imbalance: all of these dualistic concepts are shaped and woven by our myths and rituals. Myths support our beliefs, and rituals give meaning to our lives. Likewise, a lack of appropriate rituals—such as for the celebration of the birth of a new child or a coming-of-age ceremony to acknowledge a young person's passage into adult responsibilities—can rob meaning from important events, causing a dismissal of their value.

I doubt if many women reading this book had a special ceremony for their first menstrual cycle. I doubt if many men had sisters who had special ceremonies. Perhaps a handful had someone tell them that now they had a special place in society and that they should be honored whenever they were experiencing the time of flow. The idea of honoring our cyclical nature is foreign in modern-day cultures. Most of us are (or have been) embarrassed if our cycles were even noticed.

By now there should be no doubt in our understanding that blood is related to power, and as such, it should be respected. Shedding blood monthly, from the indigenous perspective, gives women the power to renew themselves and society.

Given this, it would be advantageous to examine more closely the currently upheld patriarchal views of blood and power and the active presence of the male desire to own that power. Feminist author Carol Cohn remarked on the language our male political leaders choose when speaking about war in her article "Sex and Death in the Rational World of Defense Intellectuals." Such terms as *deep penetration, holes, craters,* references to the orgasmic effect of an explosion, or a country "losing its virginity" are all associated with the male desire to obtain power through sexual references connected to giving birth.[4] Even after thousands of years, the patriarchy is still diminishing the natural power of women to create, while assuming power themselves through naming destructive acts as creative.

Isn't it time we recognize that it is the divine feminine that brings forth creativity, and honor that creative power in both women and men?

5

Clearing, Cleansing, and Divine Sexuality

WE ARE NATURE BEINGS, divinely connected to Mother Earth. We govern our lives by cycles of change—day to night, spring to summer— yet we have ignored some of the most important cycles that keep our planet and ourselves in balance.

Culturally, we have lost our intuition, our ability to respond from the heart, to care for and connect with one another, and to dream together to create a world that is based on the concept of Ahimsa (do no harm.) This concept applies to harm we may do to ourselves, to one another, to other creatures, and to the planet herself. Individually, some people honor and exhibit these positive traits, but to heal our planet and ourselves, we must do this collectively as a culture. Listening to the divine feminine and returning to nature are keys to reversing these imbalances.

DIVINE SEXUALITY IS DRIVEN UNDERGROUND

In attempts to understand a culture's value system, we must not only look at the culture's behaviors but also examine that culture's creation myth. In conversion from ancient goddess cultures to modern patriarchal cultures, women were tortured and suppressed, making it dangerous for a woman to speak out against injustice of any kind. As we know, without the balanced voice of the divine feminine, patriarchy began to dominate and exploit the people and the planet. As we have also established, feminine sexuality, which was previously considered a blessing to humanity and the Earth, became threatening to men. Dismissing the importance of feminine cycles was a successful power play to insure that men were placed in positions of control. The ensuing patriarchal cultures caused a split in feminine sexuality that allowed men to determine when sex is appropriate for women and when it is not.

The reality is, however, that rules for sexual conduct should apply to both genders, and sex is best experienced within the confines of a loving, balanced, and committed relationship as a means to connect with the Divine. In this, we may join with our partners in a powerful union that brings us closer in deep communication. A marriage of soul and body is holier than a union sanctioned by church or state. Divine sexuality is a powerful avenue to higher consciousness and spiritual power. It is through holy union that we can transcend the limits of our everyday reality and enlarge our consciousness or view of life.

The Christian Church was instrumental in changing the language that defines the meaning of our myths. The word *virgin,* which actually means "one who is whole unto herself," was changed to mean "one who has not experienced sex." Thus Christian religion so reduced the divine sexuality of women that even the great Mother Mary, a divine personification of the wholeness of women, was reduced to a mythical character used to illustrate the virtues of refraining from sex. The Christian myth simply refuses to allow a spiritual woman to also be sexual because Christianity is not large enough to hold a woman as both sexual and divine.

Even Mary Magdalene, now recognized by many biblical scholars to have been the wife and disciple of Jesus, was removed from her rightful position and cast into the role of a whore by early Christian mythology.

Only in 2016 did the Catholic Church begrudgingly agree to honor Mary Magdalene as a saint whose feast day of July 22 is now officially listed on the liturgical calendar. However, the official position of the Catholic Church still disallows her true position as Christ's wife and chosen successor.

The biggest sin that occurred in the Garden of Eden was the removal and condemnation of wisdom about divine sexuality. Women were cast from the mythical garden when they were condemned for their ability to have and bring sexual pleasure. As previously implied, both parties must surrender to participate in this divine exploration of sexuality, which means the man is not totally in charge. To establish control by the Christian Church and the men who governed through the church, the new religion established a new myth, pronouncing that sex was for procreation only. It soon became a woman's duty to a man rather than an opportunity for both partners to meet and explore the Divine together.

The daughters of Eve have been wounded by allowing dysfunctional myths to create their reality. Many women struggle between trying to prove that men are wrong and dismissing male viewpoints altogether, and competing with men to prove their own worth. But the same dysfunctional myths have harmed men as well. Intelligent, sensitive, and awakened men struggle in a world of patriarchal values just as much as women do. The divine feminine in us all can lead us away from old beliefs and back to the state of cooperation that is rightfully ours.

Both women and men have propagated hurtful misconceptions through the generations. Now that we understand this, we can take responsibility to change how we think, what we believe, and how we act. We can dismiss the cultural myths in our minds and open our hearts for the divine feminine to lead us toward a greater inner wisdom. Further, we can begin to reeducate our children about the mystical possibilities of divine sexual exchange.

Young women today are as confused about sexuality as young men are. In the fight to be more like men, women have relinquished their native guidance about the appropriate sharing of sexual connection. Many modern cultures promote an appalling casualness about sex that leaves our children bereft of the joys of the true and deep connection sexual exchange can provide. I am *not* speaking here about the Christian ethic of saving oneself for marriage, which comes from a feudal system based on ownership.

I am instead speaking of inner guidance that goes beyond hormonal drives in determining when and with whom to connect sexually. I am speaking about the guidance of the heart that leads to sharing the body when deep love is present, not a child's search for love by giving her body away. Media and movies, magazines, even governments and religion fill the heads of our young people with notions of instant romance, which can only lead to disillusionment. In addition, there is no training in modern culture for using challenges in relationships as opportunities for growth. The notion of actually working through difficult situations to obtain better understanding and true connection is often disregarded in favor of the Me Generation's "I deserve this now" formulaic approach to life. We are culturally creating a generation of narcissists who are concerned about others only when it suits their own needs. We have certainly lost the reverence for the planet that sustains and supports us.

As a result of our misguided cultural constructs, sexually transmitted infections are on the rampage; unwanted children continue to pour onto an already severely overburdened planet; abortions leave young girls confused, scarred, or feeling victimized rather than feeling powerful about their choices. In addition, our ideas about what constitutes a family are rapidly changing, as families continually split apart and reform as a result of increasing divorce rates. Our disregard for appropriate ways of relating has far-reaching effects, for we have also forgotten how to relate to Earth. Lack of a respectful relationship with our planet has led to an adulterated environment that fails to adequately support life. The confusion about the way sexual exchange occurs in our culture shows a real loss of principles of the divine feminine, which stems from the Christian myth that dismisses women.

HONORING OUR NATURAL SCENTS

One of the most damning tenets of the Christian myth is that women are dirty. Both women's sexual desires and monthly shedding of blood are often considered unclean. The truth is that Eve did not sin, nor did she contaminate Adam by showing him the unity that could be achieved through divine sexuality. What Eve gave to Adam was a moment in heaven, a recognition that we are divine, and for this, both women and men were thrown out of the Garden of Eden to keep the truth secret. In the old myth, the snake came to represent fear. In the new myth, we should revere snakes, for they show us how to shed what is not needed and awaken our spirits in acts of divine surrender to one another. The creation of a new myth would return us to values of cooperation and belonging, releasing us from the current myth that compels competition with and judgment of one another.

Once the Christian myth had diminished the value of women and labeled them as unclean, even feminine scents were judged to be negative. Feminine smells reflect the cycles of life and death—grass, flowers, trees, the ocean, streams, meadows, and the fecund smell of fall leaves turning into earth. However, most Western women and men believe that feminine secretions are problematic, as evidenced by current advertising propaganda for women to cover their own natural smells with artificial douches, lotions, and perfumes.

Many men also come to believe that they will be more sexually appealing if they use artificial colognes to cover their own scents. Magazines and television programming have labeled human secretions as embarrassing, and so, we feel embarrassed. However, when we understand that our own smells are meant to guide the natural timing of our interactions, there will be no market for artificial products to sweeten our scents. Nature provides all that we need to keep ourselves clean and balanced. The repulsion of our own scents is so extreme that many women and some men are not comfortable without the application of perfume on a daily basis. And it is nearly impossible to find unscented soaps, detergents, and shampoos in a culture that promotes artificial smells. Lotions, toothpastes, deodorants, artificial douches, and even bottled essential oils cover our natural scents. Modern cultures deliver a strong message that we are neither clean nor desirable the way we are.

We have dismissed the importance of natural scents in navigating our lives. We have disregarded the research showing that, like all other animals, the pheromones of a potential mate either attract us or repel us. Instead, we have created perfumes that we believe are more pleasing than our own smells. Applying external scents will not attract our perfect biological match. Indeed, they may mask key markers about the appropriate timing of connecting, as well as how appropriate the match may be.

The obvious outcome of such behavior is that we choose a mate according to artificial smells because we have blocked our own guides: our pheromones. What happens in a marriage when couples discover that they don't care for the other's natural scent? Without the biological glue of pheromone guidance, many partners lose interest. I have often observed this in marriage counseling when clients say, "He/she just doesn't smell good to me any longer." Both women and men today have arrived at the sorry point of losing the ability to use their own smells as part of their communication. Pheromones, intended to guide us, should not be completely scrubbed away or covered over. Pheromones produced mid-cycle by women send a sexual invitation to men. Pheromones produced during menstruation signal a time for separation. Most Earth-based cultures recognize natural scents as valuable tools for guiding women and men to appropriate times for coupling or separating.

A WINDOW INTO INDIGENOUS WISDOM

As I began to learn the complexities of our biology as men and women, I became dedicated to learning more. As a result, I traveled far and wide throughout the northern hemisphere to find elders who held mystical teachings about these matters. I met with Cherokee, Blackfoot, Cree,

Crow, Navajo, Ute, Pueblo, and Swinomish native women. I spoke through interpreters to very old women who only understood their own language. I visited women in gatherings where men were forbidden to go. I spoke with African and other Earth-based women who were visiting America from their own countries. Everywhere I went I entered deep conversations about the presence of the divine feminine and a return to a collective balance by honoring our cyclical nature.

One of my favorite times of sharing occurred with a Blackfoot woman in Canada. It was summer, and the drive across Canada was beginning to feel long and hot. I decided to stop at a Blackfoot museum. I parked my car and waited for the shuttle bus to the museum. When the bus arrived, I climbed in, offering a warm greeting to the woman driver. She nodded to me and started driving. As we began the drive up the steep hill, I noticed that I was the only passenger. The driver approached the museum, passed it, and took a sharp turn leading out of the park. I sat curiously waiting to see where I was being driven, but I said nothing, respectfully waiting for the journey to unfold.

Silence filled the air, punctuated by pops and rattles as the bus made its way out into the countryside. We traveled for about twenty minutes in the quiet. Oddly, I was completely at peace about this spontaneous journey and cheerfully open to what was going to happen next. The woman driver turned and headed toward a hill in the distance. Finally, she turned to me and said, "Spirits told me to take you to our men's vision quest site. This is where our young men go to ritual quests to bring them into manhood. Here they dream and receive life guidance. We are stopping in the distance because it is a man's place. Women's places and ways of seeking visions are more private. You have questions about women. What would you like to know?"

At this surprise invitation, I eagerly told her that I was researching cycles of nature and women's menstrual customs so that I could help to reawaken the ancient traditions of treating the time of flow as a sacred time. I told her I felt that modern cultures had lost the sacred meaning of being part of nature and that I wanted to help restore the balance. I asked her to tell me whatever she wanted to share about customs among the Blackfoot women and men.

We then entered into a very deep conversation where she gave me her tribe's understanding of women's sacred cycles, the taboos established by women, the rituals taught and practiced by women, and the stories of men's respect for the power of women's bleeding. She graciously explained that the time of flow was the same as a vision quest for men: a time of purification, a time of seeking, and a time of listening to the spirits for guidance. She told me that if one listened, one could get answers not only for one's own life, but also for the whole tribe. Both men's vision quests and women's retreat during menstruation were considered sacred rituals where each gender separated themselves in order to better purify what was out of balance and to better hear what was needed to return to harmony, both in their own lives and in the lives of others for whom they prayed.

My newfound friend explained to me how important it is for women to honor the monthly time of listening so that problems don't get too big or go on for too long. She told me that it is our job as women to keep things in balance, and to encourage men to seek their own times of purification, when they, too, become aware of imbalances. If we are out of harmony ourselves, she explained, we cannot help our community maintain its equilibrium; thus are we out of balance with the Earth. She explained to me that women are the keepers of relationship, and if women do not listen to the spirits, then they do not know what needs to be done or how to do it. Both Blackfoot men and women know this and respect the wisdom that spirits offer to women during the time of flow and to men during vision quests. Both are times of sacred power. When a woman comes back from her monthly retreat, it is honored just like a man's returning from a vision quest is honored. The people want to know what wisdom the women have received.

As a Blackfoot woman matures and learns how to better listen every month, wisdom comes through more easily, and she learns how to share what she has been given—during this sacred time of deep listening—with the community. The same applies to men, as they learn how to listen during a vision quest. Both retreats accomplish the clearing of the old, the opening to spiritual guidance, and the possibility of being seeded with creative ideas for the future. The spiritual connection is very important not only for the participant, but for everyone with whom she or he shares the experience.

My Blackfoot friend told me that women used to share a place to bleed together, away from the community, but in modern times, each woman has to find her own place and way to listen. The lodges no longer exist. She did not tell me what happened to them, but I think I know. As the Christian religion moved into indigenous cultures and the idea of women's bleeding as a sacred time was erased, women were forbidden to gather together, and the women's lodges disappeared. Sweat lodges for men still exist, however, and I have noticed that women now sometimes participate in these men's ceremonies. How many women are ignoring the potency of their own sacred monthly ceremony while trying to participate in a man's ceremonial sweat lodge? Could this be another example of women trying to be men, rather than honoring the gifts of being a woman? Surely an imbalance is reflected when one gender's sacred ceremony is overlooked in favor of seeking another's.

I thanked my friend, and we began our journey back to the museum where we parted company. It was a moment of female bonding I will never forget. I cannot remember what I saw in the museum that day, but I will always remember the vision quest site and the shared conversation with a Blackfoot sister.

I was sad to learn during my travels just how much of the mystical understanding of natural cycles has been lost. I spoke to a young Crow woman who did not understand that the time of flow was anything other than something that happened once a month in order to have a baby. She shook her head when I asked about rituals or teachings about cycles and told me that in her culture, those things had long been lost. There was no one left alive who knew the secrets or the meanings traditionally passed down by the grandmothers.

I found other tribes where the Christian influence had forced women's rituals underground. At a women's gathering in a pueblo in New Mexico, I found the women hesitant to answer my questions for fear of being discovered by the men. Two grandmothers unhappily shared with me that women's lodges had been forbidden since the Christian missionaries had arrived over three hundred years ago. They told me that today, men were the only ones allowed to gather for rituals, and that the occurrence of any women's rituals was a cause for being beaten, something unheard of in ancient Earth-based cultures. They were eager to share what they remembered, while simultaneously imploring me not to let anyone know where I got the information they were passing on to me.

Cherokee and Cree people have survived the loss of women's rituals, however. While the traditional moon lodge no longer exists, the importance of separation and honoring a time of cleansing and purification during menstruation has not been lost. Women of both tribes quietly remove themselves from daily activities and allow the special time of flow to bring forth its gifts. The Cherokee recognize that change, which monthly bleeding certainly brings, can be for better or for worse, and they regard any potential change with some apprehension. Cherokee women, therefore, choose self-imposed separation during their bleeding cycle. The polarities of women and men are considered to be so opposite during a woman's cycle that women do not risk contact with the men.

Earth-based women and men have always understood the importance of honoring women's monthly sacred opportunity for cleansing. Men who are part of these cultures have respectfully watched as women withdraw to take a personal inventory, cleanse physically and emotionally, and emerge with creative ideas. Because indigenous men could see the benefit of this process yet did not have a biological opportunity for such a powerful cleanse themselves, they created special ceremonies for the purpose of their own prayer, meditation, and purification. The Cherokee men and non-menstruating women plunged into a river seven times, asking the water to take what was not needed and to give them what *was* necessary. The Plains Indians initiated the sweat lodge, a once a month purification ritual for men.

MENSTRUATION AS A TIME OF CREATIVE RENEWAL

My own adventure into ritual retreat during the time of flow surprised me by dispelling my old beliefs. I realized that retreating to a separate space during menstruation really was an idea conceived by women for women as a way of honoring the opportunity to go inward in order to then cast off whatever had outworn its usefulness.

Women shed the monthly linings of their wombs when babies are not formed, cleaning up and making way for the possibility of a new baby during the next cycle. With the sweep of unused blood, out streams a flow of emotional imbalances that may have accumulated through the month. Women are able to use their quiet separation to dream of ways to bring balance and harmony, emerging from their time of separation with new ideas for themselves, their families, and their communities. We have lost the use of this special time and its power.

Interestingly, before electric lights and birth control pills skewed our hormones, women cycled with the moon every month, going into the retreat of Nature's gift during the dark of the moon and sharing with the community during the light of the full moon. Our separation from nature has brought loneliness, uncertainty, and unhappiness, along with irregular bleeding cycles. Hiding from who we are and separating ourselves from connection to the Earth, to the sun, to the moon, to the ocean, to all things that have natural cycles is unnatural for both women and men.

Modern attitudes surrounding the fertility cycle are mostly negative. No modern-day ritual honors a young menstruant, to tell her that this is a time to develop sacred power and understanding. No rituals teach young men about their own times of listening either. We have forgotten all the reasons for personal retreats. *Purification* is a holy word.

It means eliminating what is not needed, allowing ourselves to become so sparkling clean that we have a new slate upon which to write. We have a chance to begin again—a new cycle. Purification offers a chance to expel what is intolerable, both in our own behaviors and in relationship with others. One of the most powerful benefits of purification during the time of flow could be to eliminate all the cultural pollution that surrounds such a sacred and magical time.

It would be wonderful to purge all cultural and religious beliefs that have caused women to be ashamed of their dual nature and all the misconceptions around having a bleeding cycle. It would also be a welcome change to eliminate those attitudes that have caused a rift between women and men. What ideas may be polluting your viewpoints and your own self-esteem? Do you need to withdraw into seclusion and purify your mental and emotional self to make room for the real you and to release judgments about others? I encourage each of you to examine your own needs for purification and support the return of awareness that both women and men are truly divine.

6

The Power of Words

WE ALIGN WITH the polarities of duality that are valued by our culture. From the beginning of human awareness, our reality has been based on dualistic experiences. Duality permeates every aspect of our lives, for everything on Earth has a polar opposite—dark and light, hot and cold, male and female, right and wrong, us and them. We live on a planet full of duality, yet rather than seeing opposites as different aspects of the whole, we have chosen to separate ourselves more and more through focusing on our differences. We have misused the benefits of duality by aligning ourselves with one polarity or another, leading us into traps of seeing the world in only one way or behaving according to only one set of rules. The patriarchal view values only the masculine side of our dualistic experience. One of the basic functions of the divine feminine is to see beyond the paradox of duality by blending opposites of both sides of our experience into one harmonic whole.

Under the rules of patriarchal dominance, constancy and progress became the predominant values guiding human behavior. Modern women have tried to be more like men to survive. Yet life is full of diversity and change. The divine feminine, which exists in both women and men, brings awareness of what is needed for balance, moment by moment, requiring appropriate changes during our cycles of experience.

THE ENERGY AND POWER OF WORDS

Thoughts and words have their own energy, and appropriate naming brings meaning to events. Each culture determines the prevailing meaning of an event, and accordingly gives it a name. The words we choose to explain our experiences actually contribute to creating our experience. Having chosen those words, our experiences are then defined and reinforced by our language. When our language aligns our experience with one pole or the other (as in right or wrong, strong or weak, healthy or sick) we determine the value of that experience. Therefore, before we can decide what to call something, we need to figure out what it means to us.

It's time we take a look at how we have allowed judgmental attitudes to permeate our language and thereby color our experience. The polarity of opposites in duality was never intended to cause pain and separation, and yet we have actually caused painful separation through the words we use to describe events.

Women's cycles are a prime example of how we have misused the energy of language to define and create our experiences. Many of the names modern cultures have given to menstruation have assigned a negative meaning to this event. The name we use to describe the one natural process that is part of a woman's biological, emotional, and spiritual nature determines whether we as a culture accept the gifts of the divine feminine or reject them.

Menstruation is a product of being a woman. All women have cycles of bleeding—teens, mothers, women who are not sexually active, married women, single women, professional women, and homeless women—all women, regardless of race, culture, or sexual orientation. Unless there is a medical reason preventing menstruation, all women will at one time in their lives participate in the monthly cycle of bleeding. It begins at a certain point in a girl's life and stops at a certain point after she has experienced adult womanhood. Women's biological experience perfectly illustrates that life is based upon cycles of change and informs us as to how best to use these cycles to live harmoniously in duality.

Next we will look at some of the names and terms that have been assigned to this monthly event. *Menstruation* is the medical term in English, but I am sure each of you can think of many other names you have used or heard. The words that modern cultures have chosen to describe this sacred event imply dark meanings that show just how systemic our disrespect for nature and for life has become.

TERMS THAT DENIGRATE
THE FEMININE CYCLE

Once a month women will be different than they are the rest of the month. This monthly difference marks women as being dual by nature, able to see differently and to be different according to their internal state. Dualistic perspectives are intended to give us complementary views of the world and ourselves. Since Earth is a planet immersed in duality (day and night, hot and cold, happy and sad, male and female), it would seem that women's natural duality would help guide us through the experience of living in duality. Yet that has not been the case. In cultures that value constancy, the dual nature of women has often been denied, belittled, and even dishonored. Any time something is belittled, a momentum is set in place for establishing names that reinforce the depreciation of the event. Once the demeaning name is invoked, the power inherent in the event is diminished.

Over the years I have collected cultural nicknames for menstruation, and regrettably discovered that almost all references to menstruation in modern culture have a negative connotation. Look at the ones listed below, and notice how you feel when you read them:

▾ the curse (imposed though Christian ideology)
▾ that time of the month
▾ wrong time of the month
▾ sick time
▾ monthly troubles
▾ old faithful
▾ the misery
▾ under the weather
▾ indisposed
▾ I fell off the roof
▾ the nuisance
▾ tide's in
▾ riding the red tide
▾ visitations
▾ my red-haired aunt is visiting
▾ Aunt Flow is visiting
▾ lady in red
▾ the chick is a communist (1940s jive)
▾ communists in the summer house (Norwegian)
▾ on the rag
▾ the stain
▾ period

How many of these names have an underlying meaning that infers sickness, injury, or that something is wrong with the event itself? Probably anybody who reads this can think of even more disparaging terms for women's menstruation. Even the popular term *period* infers a stopping of something and may have negative connotations in a culture that values continual forward progress. Is it any wonder that so many women have problems with self-esteem, given that the most natural of events is referred to with such names of derision and disgust? And is it any wonder that our planet is in peril with such blatant disregard for its cycles of life?

When society perceives or defines monthly bleeding cycles as being sick, injured, or wrong, women learn to devalue the duality within them. They will defensively treat the gifts of their own duality and the event of menses itself as something to be covered up, hidden, or kept secret. It becomes an event of shame because it points to an assignation of being different or weak. In turn, such cultural viewpoints become internalized into self-doubt and sabotage a woman's self-esteem. If a natural biological event can relegate a woman to a position of being ridiculed or mocked or made fun of, she is not going to want to explore the potential gifts that come with this monthly change. This kind of treatment especially affects young girls whose greatest desire is to be normal. They want to be like everybody else, and when "being normal" comes to mean not bleeding, the event is swept into secrecy or, worse, shame. The media adds to this derision of monthly bleeding by advertising that insinuates that a woman will be mortified if anyone discovers that she bleeds.

Thankfully, many aware women and men today are reexamining the negative implications that have been assigned to women's sacred bleeding and looking for the positive aspects of being a human with the capacity to see things differently at different times of natural cycles. If you are reading this book, you are probably one of the people trying to change cultural misconceptions about this beautiful event. At the very least, the book has captured your interest as a topic worthy of investigation. We have the chance to change our consciousness now, to listen to the guidance of the divine feminine, and to reassign new names to women's cycles that reflect respect for all cycles of life.

TERMS THAT HONOR THE FEMININE CYCLE

One common word used today by those who do respect women's cycles is *moontime*. The Diné refer to the time of bleeding as the time when a woman has her power. There are a few other words and terms that illustrate a connection to nature:

- ▲ woman's friend
- ▲ the flowers
- ▲ time of flow
- ▲ time of cleansing
- ▲ Mother Nature's gift
- ▲ Nature's gift

I have used *Nature's gift* and *time of flow* interchangeably with the medical term *menstruation* throughout this book because these terms expand our awareness that all cycles of life are gifts and we would do well to flow through them as they occur. Women should be able to shine the light of who they are in varying ways during different times, honoring the inherent gifts of being connected to nature.

The name *moontime* originated from Native American women who acknowledged that women's cycles reflect timing similar to the moon's cycle of change. (I discourage the use of the phrase *on my moon* because it's a cultural corruption of the phrase *on the rag,* a very negative name.) In German country districts menstruation is referred to as "the moon." French peasants call menstruation *le moment de la lune.* Menstruation is called *ngonde* (moon) in the Congo. In Torres Straits the same word means both "moon" and "menstrual blood." Many languages acknowledge the ancient relationship between women's natural rhythms and the moon's rhythms. Indeed, lunar myths provide coherent theories concerning death and resurrection, fertility and regeneration, initiation and completion.

As we delve more deeply into the exploration of the importance of cycles, I hope to change timeworn perceptions and reigning cultural assumptions about the fertility cycle. It is more than a necessary biological inconvenience required for the birth of children. Nor is it a cycle to be ignored or conquered, a dismissive view that arises from patriarchal desire to conquer and control nature. If, by the end of this book, I can convince you, the reader, to see all cycles of life as sacred, and that the names we use to describe important events in our lives deserve positive names, perhaps we can begin to change our world into a more harmonious place for us all.

7

Deep Listening

FOUR DAYS BEFORE the American holiday of Thanksgiving Day, I awakened at dawn, full of gratefulness for my heartmate, who was quietly sleeping beside me. I crept out of our bed. Making my way to the kitchen table, I grabbed a pen. All of the many things he brings to our relationship were on my mind and in my heart, and I decided to create a series of thank you notes as a Thanksgiving surprise. It's not that he had done anything unusual or out of character; I was just aware of who he was, and I was grateful. I chose different colors of paper on which to write my notes. They represented all the ways he colors and brightens my life. For days, I continued to think of more and more things about him for which I am thankful.

At dawn on Thanksgiving Day, I once again slid out of the covers and made my way to the kitchen to finish the love project I had begun. I taped my brightly colored notes to the walls all over our house. After his delighted discovery, I went for a walk by myself in the snowy, quiet morning. I could feel the presence of my guardian angels, my guides, and my spirit teachers around me as I walked, something of which I am frequently aware.

This particular morning, I smelled a sweet floral perfume as I stood in the new morning snow and marveled at the gift of spiritual guidance exuding through the smell of flowers all around me. I now recognize that smell as the presence of the divine feminine. As I walked, my thoughts became a communication with her. As I felt her wisdom enter my heart, I gained new understanding. I thanked her for her presence and help, and she gave me even more perceptions. The divine feminine was walking with me.

THE POWER OF LISTENING TO OUR INTUITION

Each of us has our own beliefs about receiving spiritual help. Some believe in guardian angels or spirit teachers; some believe help comes from Christ or the divine feminine; some believe guidance is simply the wisdom of our own intuition. I interchange the terms *guides* and *intuition,* for they are intimately connected. But whether we attribute the guidance we receive to guardian angels, to spirit helpers, to our own intuitive powers, or to the divine feminine, we cannot hear it if we do not slow down and listen. Listening, really listening, is a holy experience. It requires letting go of our preconceived ideas about who we are. It requires getting out of our own way and accepting that the guidance that comes to us is real. It requires a willingness to be divine in order to connect with the Divine.

Deeper awareness of our cyclical nature gives us a better access to connection with our intuition. Understanding timing helps us to know when to listen and when to speak. It is obvious how out of balance our daily conversations are, as we frequently interrupt one another to express our own thoughts. Often we do not allow room for a pause to consider what has been said before we hasten to express our own ideas. We have lost the natural rhythm of communication, reflecting as increased misunderstandings, even in our most cherished and important communications.

Both genders are guilty of rushing ahead with what is foremost on our minds, rather than fully listening to others. Because of their dual

Gallery Bookshop & Bookwinkle's

Mendocino, CA
(707) 937-2665
www.gallerybookshop.com

Cust: **Nichols, Lou**
EXPIRES APR 30 2018

24-Nov-17 10:55a   Clerk: staff

Trns. #: 10539181   Reg: 8

9781591437918   *Sacred Retreat: Usin*
  1 @ $16.00 $16.00

Sub-total: $16.00
Tax @ 7.375%: $1.18

Total: **$17.18**

* *Non-Tax Items*
  Items: 1   *Units: 1*

Payment Via:

CASH $20.00

Change (Cash)   **$2.82**

People say money can't buy happiness...
but you're holding a receipt from
GALLERY BOOKSHOP that tells a very
different story.

Please come again!

biological nature, women can be wonderful examples of good listeners who know when to speak. Women listen to their children; they listen to their partners; they listen to their friends. Whether they are listening to a friend pour out some deep secret, a life mate share an important goal, the small voice of a child's dreams, or the whisperings of intuition, women know that listening can make a difference. Listening is in their blood. Women also know that to really listen, they have to stop doing everything else and pay attention. It is only then that the depth of meaning is truly shared.

While we may know that the best way to hear is to stop and pay attention, we often claim that we are too busy to simply stop and do that. Even when we understand that we need to slow down, the demands of living often scream much louder than the soft voice of the inner wisdom that tells us to slow down or to stop. Nature gives women a biological opportunity to slow down and listen to their inner guidance. However, this biological urge has been culturally dismissed, while women have been programmed to put their own needs last in order to take care of others first. Our culture compels both genders to stay busy and resist any natural inclination to periodically put other duties aside and go inward to listen.

The governing myths of our culture scorn intuition as a superstition, discounting the necessity of retreating to honor our connection to unseen sources of wisdom. Our inner voice is often discounted as being unimportant or unreasonable. Far too often both women and men ignore their feelings about something or their just knowing what needs to be done without being able to explain why. No doubt each of you can count the times when you have known something and have been led to act (or not to act), yet talked yourself out of listening to your inner guidance, only to look back later and say, "I should have listened to my intuition."

Feminism arose as an effort to reestablish the balance between women and men. Yet that philosophy has actually played a part in the suppression of women's inner guidance as women have striven to be more like men in order to be considered equal. Radical feminists, seeking to compete with men, have forgotten that *equal* does not mean *the same*. They have insisted that women can do everything that men can do any time of the month. That may or may not be true, but that isn't the point. The point is, *should* we?

Women have an inner guidance system that governs the proper timing for everything. Yet the struggle to be heard in patriarchal cultures has silenced many women or caused them to ignore natural rhythms of timing. Many women today have lost their inner knowing of when to speak and when to listen. Frequently the feminine need to be heard outweighs and overrides what a woman is actually saying, while what needs to be voiced goes unspoken. Speaking too much about too little can cause an even greater dismissal by those individuals we most long to have hear us. I silently watch women engaging in empty chatter rather than carefully expressing what lies unspoken within their own hearts. Every day I see hundreds of women on cell phones; they are talking while they drive, while they walk, and while they shop. I even saw a man kissing a woman while she was talking on her cell phone. Talk about a missed opportunity! I would certainly rather be totally present with the gift of a kiss than to absently receive it while I am on an impersonal cell phone call.

The imbalance in knowing when to listen and when to speak cannot help but interfere with spiritual listening as well. It is not enough to listen to our intuition when it is convenient, or listen for spiritual guidance only when we want something. Even in prayer, many people, women and men alike, have forgotten the balance between speaking (or asking) and listening (or receiving).

We have also forgotten the link between our capacity for deep listening and our sexuality. Sexuality has been turned into a commodity in modern societies. Like everything else in our linear culture, it is focused on progress and an end result (foreplay and an orgasm). As a result, the deep listening (to our own bodies as well as to the hearts and bodies of our partners) required to make sexual exchange a divine experience is often lost, leaving many women asking if sex is even worth the effort.

Sex therapist Gina Ogden points out in her work, *The Heart and Soul of Sex,* that we have a cultural taboo against endowing our sensual, sexual pleasures with any measure of spiritual value.[1] If our sexual experiences are separate from our spiritual experiences, how can we achieve the full, wild abandon necessary for sex to be divine? If we are focused on pleasing or being pleased, we are not listening to the call to surrender that is necessary for holy union. Joining our voices in a stream of bliss through complete surrender is an excellent way to reach the Divine.

Not only have we separated our sexuality from our spirituality, we have also separated our spirituality from our daily living. Politically, environmentally, and biologically it is easy to see how we have become imbalanced through this artificial way of living. Without creating a space for listening to the Divine and to each other, we can easily become stuck in our own thoughts, habits, beliefs, and behaviors. Without deep and careful listening, we cannot detach from those patterns long enough to hear guidance, evaluate the present moment, and choose appropriate actions.

A RETURN TO THE ART OF LISTENING

The divine feminine is calling each of us to return to the art of listening, and women can lead the way by returning to the practice of withdrawing to listen during their monthly cleanse. The portal to the spiritual realm is not as open at any other time as when we are releasing what is no longer needed and listening for what comes next. With the rate of profound change that is occurring on our planet today, it has never been more important to slow down and listen before we act. Providing our own space to do so, free of distracting influences and allotting time to retreat, is important for all of us, and even more important for women, who are biologically designed with a natural urge to slow down and listen. There is a right order in the timing of every day and what each day needs from us. Yet calendar-conscious cultures dictate only weekends as times of rest, and even those days are often filled with pressing responsibilities. Our externally designated times for rest do not match our inner biological urgings to slow down at the necessary times. Artificially designated rest periods provide another indication of the many ways that we have divorced ourselves from our spiritual nature.

If we insist on moving through our days as if they are all the same, continually *doing,* we forfeit the gifts of simply *being.* This is a lesson women once shared with men, but now all of us have lost this wisdom. We cannot dwell in the space of sacred listening when we live like this. If we do not slow down to listen during the biological time we have been given for rebalancing, we imbalance ourselves by being too active, too full, too outspoken. To stay immersed in the mundane rather than using our monthly cycles as an opportunity for greater connection with Source is profane. The world would be a much brighter place if women honored this powerful time of purification and preparation. Even if we do not create a new life, deep listening during the time of flow allows our intuition to guide us in creating greater harmony, bringing new ideas, solutions to problems, and inspirations through dreams and quiet listening. Men need to create regular times for deep listening as well.

The importance of cycles can be extended to our understanding of human breath cycles. Regardless of our spiritual beliefs, we cannot live without breathing. We breathe in air for life, change it through chemical interactions, and breathe it out again, along with our energy. The breaths we release become the air of others, so we need to be very, very careful of the energy we expel. Is it full of love and acceptance, or is it full of sighs and judgment? Each of us has the same opportunity to be careful of what we release through our breathing. Positive treatment of women's cycles can model the care that is necessary when we release something no longer needed. We are all part of the cycle of life, and we need to be conscious of what we release, doing it responsibly, whether we are discharging menstrual blood, breath, words, thoughts, or everyday litter.

With the introduction of electric lights, calendar-based schedules, and more choices about whether or not to have children, women's bodies have sped up to keep pace with the complexities of modern life. Men suffer from the same fast pace of living. In many ways, our species has become more fragile; we are often more easily upset because we are so affected by the imbalances we face every day. Things such as toxins in our air and water, hormones in our food, overuse of pharmaceuticals, and the pressure to live our lives at too fast a pace take a toll on all of us. We seem to honor cultural demands of our external environment at the expense of our inner environmental needs. Humans are more sensitive emotionally and physically to the imbalances in our lives than we may want to admit.

Many people feel so trapped by the demands on them, or so inadequate in making appropriate choices for necessary changes, that they simply look for ways to numb their pain—a glass of wine or escape through a favorite television show—anything outside themselves that can serve to distract them from what they feel and what they need to do. Most people simply do not stop to listen to see what their spiritual guidance or intuition is telling them. They just keep pushing forward until they collapse into illness or sleep, or become so stressed and imbalanced that they cannot sleep at all.

Lack of deep listening can contribute to misplaced anger as well. Because we do not slow down to really listen, we are not always appropriately angry at the right thing or the right person. With increasing frequency, people are engaging in the darker facets of human behavior, expressing anger verbally or even violently out of the frustration of not having their needs met or not taking steps to meet their own needs. I am horrified that violence has become so accepted as a normal part of modern life, as evidenced in television shows, movies, and children's cartoons. Yet as imbalanced as modern life has become, there are avenues for change, if we only allow time to slow down and listen to our intuition.

There are many ways we can break the pattern of continual *doing*.

The first step is to pay attention to the fact that you are constantly attending to external duties rather than listening to your body's needs. Eat when you are hungry, not when you are nervous or upset. Food is not meant to be a comfort; it is meant to provide nourishment. When you notice that you are tired, rest. Take a bath or shower, appreciating the water. Take a walk in nature. Anything that involves spending more time in nature helps to restore balance. Walk away from the Internet and limit your use of computers. Plant a garden, feed the birds, gaze at the stars before you go to sleep. Replace florescent light bulbs with natural lighting. Change your rhythms to match nature's rhythms by waking up with the sun and going to bed early. And, most important, utilize sacred retreats in harmony with your own body's needs and cycles.

Harmony is contagious. When a woman has deeply listened while she cleared unused blood, stale emotions, and negative energy, she radiates peace and harmony that moves outward toward those around her. When she comes out of the menstrual questing place, and as the moon moves from dark to light, she also becomes full of light and energy to be used creatively for life. The faster the world moves, the more out of sync with nature we become. Yet as life has become more complicated, nature has compensated, giving women more cycles of bleeding than their ancestors (who nursed their children for longer periods of time, thereby experiencing fewer bleeding cycles) and more much needed opportunities to bring balance into their lives and the lives of their families. It is our responsibility to live in harmony with nature; if we don't, our loved ones, our children, and we ourselves are doomed.

THE RESTORATIVE POWER OF A SECLUDED RETREAT

I am not suggesting that extreme seclusion is appropriate today, yet I want to again state that designated retreat time, whether sleeping alone or simply slowing one's daily pace during a bleeding cycle, has proven to be beneficial to women and their families worldwide. I also want to reiterate that ritual seclusion practiced by women in indigenous cultures was something consistently chosen by women for women. It was not a cruel discipline forced on women by men, but rather an opportunity that women chose, even as young girls, to deepen their understanding of the mysteries of life. The wisdom of biology supports ritual separation for women during the time of flow. It is well recognized that women's hormones (FSH, LH, estrogen, and progesterone) all fluctuate monthly and are low during menses. The relationship between biochemical lows and the need to be alone during a menstrual retreat may affect spiritual experiences. It is also possible that the psychological break of time apart during menses may offer opportunities to see things with a fresh perspective.

The connection between spirituality and the body is missing in modern culture. In fact, the spiritual component has gone missing from most of our interactions, leaving a secular and insipid shell of what once were deeply meaningful connections or rituals. We have retained graduation ceremonies and church weddings, but even these are sometimes more a matter of form, lasting a very short time, rather than a lengthy experience like a vision quest or a moontime retreat that is designated for real inward change. High school graduation exercises are all that remain of coming-of-age rituals for both genders.

In *A Path with Heart,* bestselling author and Buddhist practitioner Jack Kornfield eloquently expressed the appropriateness of personal retreats for spiritual insight, saying, "Just as there is beauty to be found in the changing of the earth's seasons and an inner grace in honoring the cycles of life, our spiritual practice will be in balance when we can sense the time that is appropriate for retreats."[2] This idea pertains directly to the connection between deep listening and retreat at the right time. Designated retreat time for both men and women allows beneficial spiritual insights to develop. As we have separated ourselves from nature, modern cultures have suppressed women and denied men the understanding of how to honor our natural biological cycles. We have not been taught to honor menses as a time of the month when we are extremely receptive (to dreams, to creative ideas, to processing what is not working). Slowing down to receive guidance is important for all of us, and yet, slowing down is considered less important than being productive in modern cultures; listening has less value than speaking.

INTUITION:
A PRESENT FROM THE GODS

Spirituality and intuition are sisters. In fact, in many instances they are the same thing. Our intuition can arise from our body awareness, from patterns that our brains recognize, or from whispers and nudges from our guides or guardian angels. Intuition has been recognized in women, yet as the divine feminine returns in full force, many men are recognizing the power of their intuitions as well. Popularly called the sixth sense, intuition has also been noted as a strange or unnatural phenomenon. Yet nothing is more natural than this powerful gift of connecting with the divine feminine through nature.

Intuition should be considered a present from the gods. It is often a pure and simple result of our deep listening to the guides who are trying to help us, and to the wisdom of our bodies when they are in sync with nature's rhythms. The divine feminine is telling us that we absolutely must return to the matriarchal understanding of balance. Honoring women's bleeding cycles as a ceremony and a necessary retreat is one simple way that we can reclaim and direct the use of the sacred powers we carry in our blood. If we do this for ourselves, we do it for all of humanity.

Times of retreat are certainly not the only times we can connect to our guidance. The more we honor retreating during the time of flow (or for a man during a time of stress) the more spiritual guidance and intuition will come to us on a daily basis. When we slow down, we can hear the whisper of the divine feminine and Earth, herself, in every moment. Living this way allows us to celebrate the sacredness of life every day, not just on calendar days marked as special.

Once a year, during the Western holiday of Thanksgiving, people in Canada and America express gratitude for all the goodness in their lives. Yet how many of us tell people how much we appreciate them for who they are and what they do on a daily basis? An annual holiday offering of thanks is more beneficial if it reminds us to be spiritually thankful every day. In the same way, a monthly retreat of deep listening for guidance can remind us to listen as we move through our daily routines.

Cullen practices gratitude on a daily basis. I have had the pleasure of hearing him thank me, thank checkout clerks, and thank people on the phone for every small kindness he receives. He also sets aside time on a regular basis to be quiet and listen for guidance. He is a wonderful example of someone who practices the fine art of listening and the expressing of gratitude every day. I have come to appreciate, from living with him, how being in a state of gratitude and wonder maintains the flow of harmony and as a result, he and I share the understanding of the importance of slowing down to listen at regular intervals, and remaining grateful for the intuitive guidance we receive.

It's time for all of us to wake up and face the shadows within us. We can all reach deeply inside ourselves to connect to our own sources of guidance. To do so, we must put aside our fears, face our shadows, and move toward opportunities to connect with the divine feminine. It is possible that women can hear much needed answers for our world through intuitive listening during our biological cycles. The more women demonstrate these abilities to listen, the more men feel comfortable listening to their own intuitive voices. We are all light beings; we are all healers; we can provide spiritual guidance for our world. The divine feminine is encouraging us to return to a more balanced and natural way of living—a way that allows time for deep listening, for it is in the listening that the answers of our hearts can be found.

8

Relationships of the Heart

SEVERAL YEARS AFTER I FREED MYSELF from the prison of my
second marriage I met Cullen, my true heartmate. In the interim, I
knew instinctively that I was responsible for creating a better relationship with myself before I was going to manifest a kind and loving relationship with anyone else. I spent those years in a committed
relationship with myself. I learned to ask the right questions and to
listen to the answers that my heart whispered (or sometimes shouted)
to me. Who was I? What were my gifts? What did I need? What
fears and shadows did I need to work through and release? What
dreams guided me on my path? I journeyed through the heart, asking for guidance and listening to what the divine feminine whispered
back to me.

I left my second husband for his complete inability to see who I
was and for a failure to meet me on any level. For a while, even thinking about another relationship made me realize that I was frightened of
having someone else try to steal my spirit, disempower me, override my
needs with his own agenda, and/or disrespect me. I had good reason to
be shell-shocked about relationships, for I had been badly bruised by
disrespect. I was determined to respect myself enough to never allow
that to happen again.

WHAT KIND OF RELATIONSHIP
DO YOU HAVE WITH YOURSELF?

To start the discovery of relationship awareness, one must begin at the core. To see into the heart of relationships, we must begin with the relationships we have with ourselves. A man who was in my office for couple's therapy once asked his wife, "Do you love me more than anybody else?" From the content of their discussion, I knew he was not referring to other men, or even to family or friends. He was asking her to love him the most because he did not love himself. I knew she had done her own work when she responded, "Of course not. I have to love myself before I can love anyone else." That kind of spontaneous answer comes from the high self-esteem required for love to blossom.

My entire philosophy about love is based on knowing that if a person does not love herself or himself, does not see the wonder of who she or he is, she or he will forever be doomed to search for that special look of approval in the eyes of another. When a person loves herself or himself and is able to accept one's self completely, there is room to invite another into one's life to share a loving relationship.

Failure to love one's self, reflected as low self-esteem, is a large part of many failed relationships. How can anyone else supply a person with self-esteem? Self-esteem, by its very definition, must come from inside of one's own self. It must come from accepting who we are and loving ourselves totally, beauty and blemishes alike. Relying upon someone else to value who we are is a recipe for disaster in relationships. For women in patriarchal societies, and for men who are awakening to the divine feminine within them, it is imperative that we love ourselves first.

While it is narcissistic to love *only* yourself, it is not narcissistic to love yourself *first*. Airline attendants always instruct passengers to put on one's own oxygen mask before helping children or others. That is because if you don't take care to get the oxygen you need, you will pass out and be unable to help anyone else. The same logic applies to loving yourself. If you don't give yourself the love and acceptance you need, valuing both your talents and the parts of yourself you are working to change, you will not be able to experience unconditional love for another. You will, instead, do the equivalent of passing out from lack of oxygen.

Our culture supports the illusion of romantic longing for someone who can fill the emptiness, that special someone who can become our other half. Movies, advertising, and our cultural conditioning have incorrectly instructed us that we can fill that need with another's love. If we believe that our beloved is responsible for providing the internal feeling of being loved, we perpetuate a pattern of looking for love outside of ourselves. I recommend that if you want a healthy relationship, look for someone who is whole and who supports your being whole yourself.

OUR CURRENT,
FLAWED RELATIONSHIP MODEL

The current romantic model for relationships actually contributes to codependent thinking within relationships and may quite possibly foster increased divorce rates. It is impossible for an external source (the beloved partner) to continuously provide the necessary stream of love endorphins we need for our own self-regard, and it is exhausting for him (or her) to try. Think of how tiring it is to continually try to make someone else happy when they are unable to access their own inner happiness. Asking someone else to be responsible for our happiness is an unfair request to anyone we truly value and love, for the other person cannot attend to his or her own internal needs if he or she constantly has to monitor ours. How can that be a balanced relationship of any real duration? Emotional exhaustion and lack of self-growth lead both partners to either resign themselves to getting less than they deserve or to look for another source to supply the high of being in love.

In our culture, there is no room to examine our shadow. Personal retreats provide opportunities for self-assessment and for making whatever changes are necessary to accept and love ourselves more. If our culture valued regular private retreats, the insights that arise during these powerful times, and the creative solutions that likewise arise from dark internal places, perhaps we could break the vicious pattern of thinking that suggests we need to be perfect. Our views of perfection have become rigidly determined by an artificial value system. Mistakes in our culture are rarely seen as avenues for growth wherein if we make a mistake, we learn from it. Our partner makes a mistake, and he or she learns from it. Together we grow.

Because of our societal emphasis on perfection and constancy, however, couples find themselves baffled by the natural cycles present in *all* relationships. And yet we must learn to recognize that relationships have cycles just like everything else—there are times of sharing and times to do things on our own. There are times that we are clicking on all cylinders and can share what we are thinking with just a glance, and times when every word we utter seems to be misconstrued by our partner. Many couples question if they are in the right relationship during these times of disconnection. In societies that promote constancy and fairy tales that end with "and they lived happily ever after," we have all been led down a path that not only does not exist, but also would be boring if it did! I would love to hear the fairy tale that ended with "And they continued to change and grow together for the rest of their days!"

Unfortunately, too many of us in the bliss of new love fall into believing that our loved one is perfect, only to be sorely disappointed when he or she disagrees with us or makes a little mistake. It follows also, that if we expect our mates to be perfect, we want to be seen as perfect ourselves. So when we make a mistake, or when we move into the dark phase of our personal cycles to wrestle with our own shadows, our self-esteem drops, and we may struggle to accept love that is offered. This is very likely because we do not, at that moment, love ourselves enough.

It's dangerous to desire perfection within ourselves or to project that our loved one is perfect, although they may indeed be the perfect partners for us. Indeed, telling someone else that they are perfect assigns them the task of having to live up to *being* perfect. How tiring. And what a time bomb for conflict!

Good relationships are born out of understanding that we are connected even when we disagree; we must respect our differences as well as our likenesses. No single way of being human is perfect, and it is the beauty of our differences that causes our initial attraction to one another. We are all parts of one human family, one body, like drops of water in the same ocean. Approaching relationships from this angle allows each of us to be imperfect beings moving toward our more whole and future selves. With the one special person we choose, the one who is not perfect, but again, who is perfect for us, we can work from a mutually shared world view to help each other grow.

A FALSE VIEW OF THE PERFECT MATE

Relationships are important to all of us, regardless of gender. Yet cultural assumptions and our acceptance of false advertising have tarnished our views of relationship. Marketing and fantasy movies have led most women (and men) on wild goose chases, pursuing romantic notions that have little to do with deep relationships or real and unconditional love. Many people believe that they must use manufactured charms (lily-white smiles, artificial smells, fake breasts, clothes that make a certain statement) to capture the essence of love. Some even judge the importance of a relationship by the size of an engagement ring. Yet such surface charades create relationships that have no depth. And although most men appreciate beauty and sweetness, and most women appreciate strength and good looks, a person of deep character will not be drawn to someone who is using artificial tricks (clothing, colognes, etc.) for long.

Even our sexuality has been deeply tarnished in modern cultures through conflicting messages. Media throws sex into our faces to sell cars or vegetables, while religion takes the stance that sex is appropriate only under the guidelines of the church. Women today are often confused, feeling they are lacking if they don't have active sex lives and condemned if they do. It is not the focus of this book to address that issue, yet it is so deeply a part of what is out of balance, that I must mention it, if only peripherally.

There is a joke that states that men talk to women in order to have sex with them, and women have sex to talk to men. Sadly, there is some truth in this saying. Many people today engage in sex in an effort to find intimacy and connection. But that is painfully backward! Most often, modern men and women link sex to intimacy and actually believe that if they are having sex, then they are being intimate. However, this is a romantic ideal that, sadly, is far from being true.

Intimacy and sex are not the same thing. Sex can come from real intimacy, but sex is not necessarily intimate, although it should be. Intimacy is being completely comfortable with being who you are in the presence of another person. Why would you share your body with someone that you don't feel you can be yourself around? It would behoove us to address our assumptions about intimacy and sexuality to understand the importance of exploring true intimacy before we explore sexuality, for sex without intimacy is shallow and sad, and often focuses only on performance, not connection. In *The Heart and Soul of Sex,* therapist Gina Ogden points out that "performance sex" tends to bypass our feelings and the meanings attached to sexual sharing.[1] It also bypasses our deep connections with the rhythms of the planet. Need I say more?

We need more connection, not more sex. The reason so many women love to dance (and often bemoan the fact that they can't get their partners to dance with them) is because they are seeking connection. In their work *The Wise Wound,* British poet and author Penelope Shuttle and her husband, fellow British poet and author Peter Redgrove, point out that the accented rhythms of dance play an important part in activating the feminine style of consciousness, as it puts women in touch with their own body rhythms.[2] Women inviting their partners to dance are offering to share their life rhythms with them. Men who are afraid to dance are often afraid they will perform poorly. What they fail to realize is that the best performance they could achieve has very little to do with proper dance steps. It has to do with the act of sharing respective rhythms, for by sharing rhythms, true connection is achieved.

GUIDELINES FOR CREATING A SUCCESSFUL RELATIONSHIP

There are several important ingredients that are important to achieve true and deep connection in any relationship. One of the most vital is transparency, wherein we are willing to be seen for who we really are; we cannot hide behind illusions we project or what we perceive to be a better image of ourselves. True transparency is necessary for communication, sexual connection, and growth, and to experience the unconditional love that is possible when we allow another to see our most painful places and the shadows that we are working to change. Transparency with one another is an absolute must in any healthy and fulfilling relationship.

The larger human understanding of depth and commitment in relationship has been all but lost in today's confusing social mores that honor biological imperatives and competition for equality without regard for real caring, intimacy, and connection. The Women's Liberation Movement and other feminist philosophies have twisted female-male interaction away from nature in a misunderstood striving for equality. This imbalance is clearly reflected in rising promiscuity in both women and men.

The idea that sex can be used to feel good, gain an advantage, or for shallow fun erodes any possibility of deep communication between genders, forcing many of our young people into hardened roles of anticipated failure, accompanied by attitudes that can only be described by the words, "Get what you can, because nothing lasts." Such attitudes show little respect for a process of right timing and the gradual unfolding of what might be an introduction to the real thing. Internet and the transmission of instant information lead to the further expectation among young people that they deserve instant gratification, including instant information, instant human connections, and instant orgasms. Deep connection does not happen like that, but many of our young people living under the current myths are caught in the illusion that they are (or should be) living the good life, having a good time, and experiencing true freedom. One day, however, they may wake up to the fact that they are consumed by a pervasive sense that something is missing and that life is not, after all, so grand. They may feel disconnected and alone. Suicide is on the rise in young people, a clear warning that our cultural messages are out of balance.

WHAT DEFINES A "FAIR FIGHT"

Another important ingredient in a successful relationship is being able to disagree, or if necessary, to fight fairly. The conflicts in which we engage from our differing points of view become the fodder for our growth. If disagreeing is necessary (and often it is in order to share different views), it is imperative to be an honorable warrior, lest you injure the person and relationship you hold most dear. It is important to know how to fight with integrity.

First, we must recognize the enemy. That seems obvious, but it isn't always so apparent when we feel caught in a welter of conflicting emotions. While sometimes the enemy actually is the person standing in front of us (if we are in an abusive or narcissistic relationship), more often the enemy is the *misunderstanding* between us. In healthy relationships, the enemy is the discord, not the person. To restore harmony, it would be prudent to identify and address the essence of the discord, with each person being allowed to fully express his or her viewpoint without judgment or blame.

The second component of fighting with integrity is compassion. It is absolutely necessary to be compassionate in the middle of battle in order to respect each person's integrity and to preserve the relationship.

We must have compassion for the other's feelings. Compassion does not mean that you give in to the other side. It is a simple acknowledgment that the other person must be feeling some discomfort, distress, or emotional pain, or they would not be doing what they're doing or saying what they're saying. Compassion requires listening with an open heart, sharing with an open heart, and not reacting to what is being heard or shared. In the midst of a disagreement, it helps to not only listen to the other point of view, but to also sense the other person's pain. Acting and reacting with compassion allows your heart to release its grip of anger and soften toward resolution.

A third factor is strength. Being strong is not the same as being obstinate. There is gentleness in real strength, as any gentleman's behavior will demonstrate. Being strong is recognizing when to insist on being heard and when to yield by listening. In the cycle of an argument, there is a space for both. If you find it is not possible to do both, it is not a fair fight. Fighting with integrity requires combining gentleness with strength and refusing to forfeit one for the other.

A fourth ingredient is paying attention to our thoughts during the disagreement. What are you thinking about yourself or about the other person when you are in the heat of battle? Continually repeating to yourself, "He is such a jerk!" or "I will never understand this!" is not helpful. Such thoughts are merely expressions of your frustration, and continually repeating them only further assigns your partner the role you expect him to play.

When I am in this situation, I find it productive to focus my thoughts on a positive outcome, such as, "I know I can say what I need to say with kindness" or "I know he wants to understand me" or "I know he loves and respects me even when we disagree." Such thinking removes me from the carnage of battle and keeps me steady on my path as an honorable person who occasionally needs to disagree. If you continually feel you need to change your partner's behavior, you may wish to begin thinking, "I am not responsible for his (or her) bad choices." These thoughts encourage you to release any desire to control your partner.

A fifth component of healthy disagreements is the value of timing. Military leaders use timing to look for advantage, a chance to catch the enemy off guard. This type of timing is the timing of war, and it does not work in relationships. A person fighting with honor and integrity looks for right timing as an opportunity to bring resolution. Fighting with honor is not about proving your point or making the other person wrong. Fighting with honor requires that you preserve the integrity of the other's self-esteem during the battle, not destroy it with your emotional outbursts, even when you believe them to be justified. Timing in battle is important. It is not the time to engage in battle when one partner is feeling down or discouraged. Nor is it good timing to blast your mate with your viewpoint when you are overwrought with emotion. It is kinder in both situations to say, "Let's discuss this later" or "I am too angry and hurt to talk about this right now. Can we discuss it in a few hours, or perhaps tomorrow?" Honoring the right timing to resolve a disagreement is one of the ways we can respect healthy cycles in relationships. There is a time for everything, and being flexible to allow the right timing to unfold creates greater opportunities for harmony.

These five ingredients for honorable arguments within personal relationships can be applied to *all* relationships. The key for making the formula work is that both partners must play by the rules of fair fighting, and both must act with inscrutable integrity. If both partners do not play by the rules, there will be wounds that may be difficult to heal or relationship carnage. Asking for forgiveness later may be inappropriate and too late.

Integrity in relationships requires being who we are in the face of adversity. That means not caving in out of guilt at your own imperfections, nor being angry with another for what you perceive as *their* imperfections. Proper timing calls for withdrawing when emotional flags are raised, alerting you to an existing imbalance. These emotional flags are raised to focus your attention on changes that need to occur, usually within yourself or with how you are responding to outer circumstances and other people. Personal assessment of your own emotions prevents irritating issues from building to a point of insurmountable conflict.

The indigenous idea of separation during menses created a natural rhythm of withdrawing and coming together within relationships. Withdrawing is appropriate for both men and women any time intense emotions are involved in a disagreement. A walk in the forest can help us do our own inner work before engaging our partner in battle. We not only protect the relationship from harmful emotions that first need to be processed within ourselves, we also gain the opportunity of deeper insight and creative ideas about how to do things differently.

DETERMINING WHAT WE WANT IN RELATIONSHIPS

Disregard for the natural rhythms of women's cycles has led to women being unsure of how to navigate their inconsistencies. There is a cultural problem inherent in accepting that it's a woman's prerogative to change her mind and indeed, this construct often interferes with harmonious relationships. Many women (and the men who live with them) suffer from what a woman may consider as the right to change her mind, which instead might simply be an inability to determine how to make a correct choice. To help with decision making, it's important to heed the cycles of the body and an intuitive following of the heart at all times.

The retreats I suggest in this book may facilitate this, for they are capable of offering a way to find new perspectives. Some people may find that they enjoy a retreat so much that they continue this pattern of separating and coming together in a rhythmic manner even after one's biological cycles have ceased. Being in a relationship gives us the chance to test what we have learned when we are by ourselves. It gives us opportunity after opportunity to live in challenging circumstances and move past our own fears and our own shadows. For whenever we are unhappy emotionally, a very big part of that emotion is really a reflection of how we see ourselves.

Sometimes the choice of being true to ourselves overrides the choice of being in a particular relationship. If one is in a wounded state as a result of a breakup, this may be the perfect time to withdraw and examine what you want and to make some conscious choices about your life. Most people focus on what they don't want when they are recovering from a breakup. But that is only part of the process. The larger, often overlooked part is to determine what one *does* want.

Out of curiosity, I took a poll of my women friends, asking, "What to you is the number one most important thing in relationship?" Below are the reported requirements, in order of popularity of response:

1. Trust
2. Compatibility
3. Honesty
4. Respect
5. Acceptance
6. Responsibility for words, actions, and choices
7. Partner having their own identity

It's interesting to me that not one single woman named love as an essential element in an important relationship. Perhaps these women knew and understood that true love is based upon all of these other qualities. Or perhaps they have eliminated love from their list because of cultural misunderstandings about love. To my way of thinking, it's important that unconditional love be present for a successful intimate relationship, for without love, the very heart of the relationship is missing. Without love, the heart is not open to sharing. Without love, all the other shining attributes pale.

Another important thing jumped out at me as being missing from the above list: sex or passion. I was shocked to discover how many women have settled for passionless relationships or traded their desire for sexual connection for having other types of needs met.

People often hurry from one relationship to the next in a desperate search for love or companionship, leaving out the necessary part of the cycle that allows for introspection and examination of what they have to offer and what they need. I have noticed that most women who are not in relationship are looking for a relationship. The ones who are not looking are often so damaged by previous relationships that they are sometimes too frightened to even consider a male friendship. There is great value in taking time to create a relationship with ourselves before looking for a deep relationship with another. If we don't honor the times of solitude, how can we know who we are or what we really need? None of us are the same person at the end of a relationship that we were at the beginning, and often we need to heal a few wounds as well as assess our strengths before we can move on. Once we have done a thorough inventory of our own internal state, attributes, needs, and desires, we can then spend time listing the things we need in our next relationship, asking such valid questions as:

▲ "What is essential to my happiness?"
▲ "What do I need to thrive?"
▲ "What makes me laugh?"
▲ "What makes me feel safe"
▲ "How do I recognize that I'm being respected?"
▲ "What makes me feel accepted and loved unconditionally?"

Once we have the answers to these questions, we can look for these traits in people we meet, rather than trying to romanticize others.

It would also be useful to examine what *we* bring to a relationship by asking questions about ourselves, such as:

▲ "What can I contribute to a relationship?"
▲ "How can this person benefit from being in relationship with me?"
▲ "Do I respect this person and honor what is important to him/her?"
▲ "Can I accept this person and love him/her unconditionally?"

▲ "Can I support this person's path of evolution as he or she grows and changes?"

An important step in choosing the right partner is to examine that person's world view. One predictive value of success in a relationship is that both partners hold a similar world view. That means that you share the same values, same priorities, same expectations, and same beliefs about life. Within that world view there is much room for individual preferences, goals, and opinions. Those differences are what make the relationship interesting! Carbon copy opinions are not what we're seeking. Instead, we're looking for the ability to respect differences of opinion within the relationship, while sharing the same global view on important issues, including spiritual beliefs, money and time management, views about family and children, and environmental concerns, for instance.

My own list of absolute essentials for relationship was devised during lengthy times of retreat when I was not in an intimate relationship. Each person should have her own list of requisites, but in my opinion, if the list doesn't contain respect you might want to rethink it. For women, lack of respect is so endemic in our culture that many women, in the ardor of being pursued, often fail to see that it's missing. When the roses arrive, accompanied by smooth and silky words, desire for connection often overrules the warnings we might otherwise notice. Two more values to be considered for inclusion on the list are honesty and good communication. A relationship won't go far without these three.

If you are evaluating a potential partner, notice how he or she treats others (grocery store clerks, friends, other women, other men, siblings, business partners). Does he or she show road rage? Is he or she kind to animals? How they treat others may be an important clue to how they will treat you.

Before I met Cullen, I consciously retreated to examine who I was, what I had learned, and what I had to offer, as well as what I wanted in a relationship. I took my time and thoughtfully, soulfully, created my list. About two years after my list was made, my ideal partner appeared, and we now joyfully share a loving, passionate, and transparent relationship. I met him at an art gallery. It was so obvious to me that he was special and different that I invited him to go for a walk. When he immediately said yes, I was delighted.

After our walk, we sat under a new moon and talked, and although I was afraid to acknowledge what my heart was telling me, inside I knew there was something extraordinary between us. I had dreamed about meeting a special man, but I did not look for him. I simply waited until the universe provided the moment and the opportunity. Still, I dragged my feet (failing to give him my telephone number). Through months of letter writing, my heart slowly let go of its fear and moved toward accepting love. Eventually I was ready to accept the gift I was being given. After almost seven months of corresponding by writing letters only, which established transparency and intimacy between us, we moved quickly and flawlessly into a true partnership. Our partnership was and is marked by unconditional love and a shared commitment to our divine growth and evolution.

Our relationship is deeply spiritual, deeply connective, passionate and fun, full of growth, and it is obvious that we were meant to be together. If I had to go through all of the lessons I endured (and apparently I did) in order to arrive at this incredible union, life with Cullen is a fabulous reward! Because I learned from each experience, because I took time to work with my own shadows, I reached the place of becoming whole and was able to meet a partner who was also whole, balanced, and wonderful.

Below is the list I made years ago of what I needed in an intimate relationship. It remains true today. Bear in mind, please, that unconditional love is the ultimate quality required for all relationships, and should be at the top of any list. But before that love blooms, while it is blossoming, look for any of these other qualities that are important to you:

- respect (for himself or herself, for you, and for all of life)
- honesty
- transparency
- total trust
- kindness (not just to you, but to all of life)
- compassion
- integrity
- shared world view (including spiritual beliefs, goals and dreams, expectations, and/or how to deal with challenges)
- love of nature
- love of silence
- love of beauty
- health consciousness
- good communication (two-way listening, and speaking with kindness, clarity, and no judgment)
- desire to explore sexuality as a deeper form of connection and communication
- generosity of spirit, time, and possessions
- loyalty and devotion
- understanding
- acceptance (even when he/she does not understand)
- good boundaries with appropriate sharing
- strength of character
- ability to know himself/herself
- desire to grow and change
- courage to grow and change
- willingness to work with his/her shadows
- confidence in himself/herself
- confidence in me
- willingness to teach me
- willingness to learn from me
- desire to make a difference in the world
- desire to be of service to others

▲ care for the environment

▲ ability to discuss problems without blame or judgment

▲ sensitivity to timing

▲ willingness to compromise

▲ independence balanced with a desire to share

▲ wise balance of when to place himself/herself first and when to place others first

▲ ability to follow his/her own interests

▲ willingness to explore new things with me

▲ willingness to dance with me

▲ sense of humor

▲ ability to laugh at himself/herself

▲ ability to laugh at circumstances

My list requires that my partner have the soul of an artist—to be able to see the beauty of the world and to love it with passion. Obviously, sharing all of these things brings the ability to enjoy each other's company. The most essential and valuable requirement on my list is that my partner cherishes our relationship and me, even when the world seems like a harsh or unfair place, and is grateful for my presence in his life. With these essentials in mind, and with my meeting the requirements on his list, our relationship is exquisite.

OTHER MARKERS ON THE ROAD TO A HEALTHY, FULFILLING RELATIONSHIP

Take a look at any women's magazine today, and you will see that relationship issues are still the number one area of interest. From deep within our bodies, women understand timing and connection, and that understanding extends to enhance our relationships. With women's natural interest in relationships comes our sacred task to tend to relationships. Not that by any stretch we should ever take the sole responsibility for any relationship, but we must recognize that the urge for our connections to grow is part and parcel of our natural feminine inclination to share our hearts. We must also recognize that often, when men approach us sexually, they are seeking connection. Balanced men understand that connection with their partners, not a sexual climax, is the ultimate goal of sex.

Relationships are like plants that need water, sunshine, and light; they require effort. If one partner feels that the relationship is not working, there is an implication that the other partner is unaware or unwilling to do the required work of tending the relationship. And relationships have cycles, just like every other living thing. Every partnership needs space. Withdrawing to process and evaluate while nurturing ourselves helps us to replenish the well so that we can come back to our respective relationships full again—full of love, positive self-regard, respect for others, creative ideas, and the ability to offer ourselves for service to community. If we don't allow ourselves this opportunity, we can become trapped by the choices we make.

There are times in any relationship when tears are appropriate; tears are cleansing and can help to clear out problems and lubricate the way for solutions. That said, tears should be directly related to going inward and compassionately looking at our own lives to see what we need to change. Tears are not supposed to be shared simply because we are upset and frustrated. Again, strong emotions are tools to be used. They are our guidelines to what is out of balance. Acting on our emotions requires making changes within ourselves. We can never change anyone else. It is appropriate to be angry about injustice or to be sad at disappointments. But we should evaluate these emotions and their messages internally before we act on them externally. We can use our personal time to temper our anger and channel it to needed directions or use our sadness to release something (or someone) that is no longer working in our lives.

Once, in a counseling session, a woman told me her story through tears of realization. She poured out words that had been stuffed inside of her for such a long time that they could no longer be contained. She was trapped in an unhappy marriage, which she had chosen out of guilt. Angrily she told me:

> For thirty-six years I have been married to the wrong man. I was seventeen, and I knew what was right and what was not but I didn't listen to my inner voice. I started having asthma when he was around. My body told me to break up with him but I didn't. When we were dating, I let my guard down, and he touched me when my body didn't want him to. I knew better. I received warning signs, but again I didn't listen to them. Then I felt guilty because he touched me inappropriately, and I let him. I'd known better, but I hadn't stopped him. I felt so guilty about it that I married him. Thirty-six years later, no matter how hard I try; I can't get him to listen to what is important to me. I should have listened to my own inner feelings.

This woman spilled her sorrow like a swollen river climbing out of its carefully held banks. She is a tragic example of a woman who did not listen to the messages of her body, found herself locked into an unhappy relationship for thirty years, and didn't understand that she had the power to change it. What we feel in our bodies can guide us through appropriate changes in ourselves or in our interactions with others.

TIME-OUT TO PROCESS ONE'S EMOTIONS

Relationships are miraculous opportunities for growth and change. Indigenous elders knew that change was the secret of life. Diné women call the creator of life Changing Woman, because life is continually changing. Women elders taught that recognizing and honoring women's inherently changing nature positively affected all relationships and showed them how to navigate life more successfully. This is why they created the time of separation for women to honor the changes that come, the lifting of the veil between realities to allow better sight, and the opportunity to grieve and get angry without having those emotions create toxicity in their relationships. The moon lodge, a place for ritual separation designed by and for women, offered a place to honor the emotions that arise to show us the way during our cycles.

In my doctoral research I interviewed men whose partners were sleeping apart from them during their menstrual cycles. I wanted to know what the men experienced from their mates' withdrawal once a month. Many men agreed that it was a purposeful and positive new step in their relationships. Most shared with me that when their partners started using the time of flow as a private time for introspection, they as a couple learned how to fight in a healthier way. One man said to me, "Now I know why she has been mad at me for the last seventeen years."

Women often avoid conflict because of an intense desire for harmony; there is a fear that expressing dissatisfaction will cause such disequilibrium in the relationship that it will never recover and may actually be lost. Sometimes this happens. But more often the fear of conflict promotes the suppression of what is not working, or worse, the sharing of complaints with others, rather than working on them within the relationship. When this happens, dissatisfaction leaks out in other ways that can poison the very relationships we hold dear. Having a ritual separation offers an opportunity for emotions such as anger and sadness to emerge in a safe way and a chance to really sit with those feelings until they are emptied. Once emptied of the negative emotions, something else can come in—something mystical and wonderful: guidance about what we can do next and how to do it.

THE POWER OF FORGIVENESS

One thing we have not addressed is the aspect of forgiveness in relationships. It takes a loving heart to forgive, and it takes complete honesty and compassion with ourselves and with our mate to be able to forgive. We would be wise to accept that our little mistakes (and some of our big ones) are teaching tools to make us better human beings. We must be gentle with ourselves and equally gentle with our loved one when either of us makes a mistake. In a healthy loving relationship neither partner ever intends to hurt the other, yet we make mistakes just the same. Repeated mistakes often give us different vantage points of a challenge until we understand how to do things differently. This is how we grow. When we understand this premise, there's nothing to forgive; everything is seen as an opportunity for growth.

Frequently we get our feelings hurt because we believe that our loved one does not love us enough or in the right way, or else he (she) wouldn't have done (said) that. If we change our belief, we may be able to see the true cause of the problem. It could be that our mate does not love or respect us enough to prevent whatever did or did not occur. But it could also be true that our mate simply did not understand the importance of the event to us, or how to do things differently. It's helpful to remember that our partner doesn't mean to hurt us when he or she says or does something that doesn't match our hopes or expectations. It's also helpful to be clear about our own thoughts and actions, so that we always do the best we can in every moment. And we might try to remember the rules of honorable fighting. If we live our lives like this, there is usually very little to forgive.

THE SACRED TRUST OF PARENTING

I have a few special things to say about relationships with children. Sometimes parents try to mold their children into their own view of what their children should be. By giving birth (or adopting), these parents invest themselves in the outcome of the child's development. A parent may begin to think that the behaviors of the child reflect his or her skills as a parent or his or her worth as a human being. I would like to encourage all parents to understand that the sacred trust of parenthood does not require that you mold your children in any particular direction. Rather, the task seems to be to shape the relationship and provide a safe container in which they may grow into who they are meant to be. If you guide them in the skills of being in relationship (with you, with siblings, with friends, with the Earth, and with all life) and help them to understand that all relationships have cycles, as do all living things, you will have given them the greatest gift possible besides your love. All relationships flourish by following the same guidelines. Respect, honesty, transparency, communication, kindness, compassion, integrity, and a little laughter produce loving relationships. Are these not values that we want to use in relationship with our children, our friends, and even in relationship with Mother Earth?

A real honoring of natural cycles can lead to a greater awareness of the possibilities open to us all. The beginning of a cycle returns to the end, to begin again. Each spiral adds another dimension, for as the cycle continues there is vertical movement as well, which brings our consciousness to increasingly higher levels. Cycles are important to help us understand how everything is connected and allow us to move away from old patterns of conflict caused by pushing against our perceptions of polarized differences. If we ignore natural cycles, we may never reach the higher conscious awareness that these gradually increasing spirals of wisdom can provide. This is why women and men who are led by the divine feminine are so often peacemakers and caregivers. The divine feminine knows that life is about change, and movement brings understanding, resolution, possibility, and peace, peace, peace.

9

Dreaming Cycles

THE DREAM JOLTED me upright. I was not sure which was the reality, me in my nightgown rubbing my eyes or me walking on a trail in the brilliant sunlight. I was in my private space, on my own experiment with sacred retreat during Nature's gift. While I have always been an avid dreamer, the clarity and intensity of this dream was a complete surprise to me. It was startling.

I dreamed I was walking down a trail in the woods when I encountered a bear and a mountain lion. While I had dreamed of these animals separately in the past, I had never encountered both of them in the same dream. Additionally, each time I had previously dreamed of either, it had been very clear to me that they had come into my dreams to help me.

This dream, with both animals in it, terrified me, for they approached me and began to rip the flesh off my bones. They persisted until I was completely consumed, and then they spit me out in a new form. I watched myself disappear, and my terror vanished as the dream animals gave me new life. With the new arrangement of my bones in the shiny new skin of my dream body, I proceeded down the trail until I came to a hidden waterfall. I approached it, stretching out my hand to touch the shimmering, azure water. In the dream, I noticed my hand

and the water were the same—transparent, sparkling, and beautiful. This was a new and key understanding for me. I was connected to the water. I wakened from that dream a different person.

It took days for the magnitude of that dream to sink in. I realized that I knew things about the world that I hadn't known before. I understood in a clear and direct way that I was a divine part of nature; I was connected to everything much more deeply, and I could see the connection. My heart was full of compassion. I realized that I had experienced what many call a shamanic dream, one that broke me apart and put me back together in a whole and holy way. The dream and the spirit animals that came to help me appeared during the time and in the space that I had made sacred by preparing for my personal ceremony of cleansing and renewal during the time of flow. I was rewarded. My spirit helpers cleaned me up, renewed my understandings, and showed me who I really was! The power of this dream showed me the sanctity of Nature's gift in my own life, and I wanted to share it with others. I knew that it was important to withdraw into myself to purge, receive, and create, and for me, dreaming was part of this whole process.

While my dreams have always been vivid, they have also been unpredictable. Sometimes I have dreams that process my day, or work out some troubling issue in my life. Sometimes they are prescient dreams, informing me of possible dangers or opportunities. I never know what type of dream will arrive in the night.

This dream had come at a specific phase of my bleeding cycle. I had recorded my dreams for some time, and now I decided to note the time of month my dreams occurred. I noticed with great interest that the deeply insightful dreams only occurred if I allowed the time and space for guidance by sleeping alone in my own sacred space. I also noted that these really insightful dreams were also more frequent during my time of flow. Apparently what my Blackfoot friend had told me was absolutely valid. Sleeping alone to quest for insight during my own bleeding cycle had brought me a vision and a new understanding of how to approach life. In the years since my bleeding cycle stopped, I have continued my solitary retreats in connection with the moon, listening and asking for guidance. The practice still rewards me with potent and meaningful dreams.

Researchers have classically defined dreams as symbols, images, sounds, sights, smells, tastes, and motor activities that occur during sleep to process daily experiences. Shamanic understanding extends the definition to include the wisdom of non-ordinary reality that arrives when our ordinary consciousness has been laid to rest. People vary a lot in their need for sleep. Some dream researchers have suggested that when a portion of oneself is not integrated into awareness, more time must be spent in dealing with it separately in the dream state. According to this view, it could be implied that dreaming helps integrate a person's awareness, and spiritual dream experiences may enhance that integration. Shamanic dreams come more readily if we prepare for them and create a sacred space for the dream guides to visit us.

DREAM BELIEFS OF INDIGENOUS PEOPLE

In a cross-cultural comparison of dreaming among sixteen Native American tribes, noted American psychologist and parapsychologist Stanley Krippner and April Thompson determined that each of the investigated cultures placed key values on dreams. In most of the Native American models, it was found that the dream often represented the dreamer's merging with the unknown visionary realm, which can enlighten and empower the dreamer.[1]

In Native American cosmology it is understood that the spirit world is the source of dreams. In *Woman as Healer,* psychologist Jeanne Achterberg takes a similar stance about allowing boundaries to merge in order to receive guidance. She shares that the mystic experience that brings knowledge and insight from sources beyond can only happen if the barriers separating the self from the nonself become fluid and the imagination reaches beyond the intellect.[2]

Prevalent North American indigenous beliefs about dreams may be summarized as follows:

Mojave: Dreams are the link between human beings and the spiritual world;

Kwakiutl: Dreams represent direct contact with spiritual realms;

Crow: Dreams come from the spirit world. The dreamer is in communication with the spirit world;

Blackfoot: Dreams are produced by dream spirits who manifest as messengers, often in animal form. These dream spirits appear to bestow valuable gifts or information;

Maricopa: Spiritual power comes only in dreams;

Objibwa: All knowledge is the result of dreams.

Australian Aboriginals believe that there is a link between dreaming, blood, and the perceivable world. The body needs the nourishing energy of the blood to maintain itself, and the blood purportedly needs subtle energies from the spirit world, which is attained through dreams. Recognizing the dream connection between energy from the spirit world and the physical body's energy maintains the communication between them. Based on this indigenous view of the connection between blood and dreaming, one could conclude that the content of one's dreams is a valuable asset.

POTENT DREAMS DURING MENSES

As we have established elsewhere, it has been shown that women have more vivid and more meaningful dreams during menses. My original study yielded important insights about when and how women can most easily receive dream guidance. Dreams during Nature's gift may be more useful to women and to their communities because women can receive more inspiration, illumination, creative ideas, and/or spiritual guidance during this potent time if they have a private, sacred space for dreaming. There is a relationship between the level of estrogen in a woman's body and her frequency of dreaming, as well as her dream recall.

Understanding our dreams and being able to follow their guidance is to accept the validity of our emotional experience. What is the emotion in the dream telling us? This theory needs to be explored more deeply, for understanding the cyclical timing of women's dreams could lead to important discoveries for all human dreaming. Men receive important guidance in dreams, too, yet there has been no research to date supporting hormonal influence upon men's dreaming. If women's dreams are more potent during certain hormonal phases and when honored in a spiritual space, certainly the timing of men's dreams deserves equal investigation and respect. Until that research happens, we can begin our own investigation by working with the emotions that accompany messages within the dream state.

MORE INSIGHTS INTO THE DREAMING WORLD

Emotional signs are pretty clear: a negative emotion indicates we should move away from a situation; a positive feeling encourages us to continue in a particular direction. If we are upset by a dream, it has something instructive to tell us; the dream is telling us to make a change. If we are happy from a dream, we can surmise that we are being encouraged to continue on a certain path. We would benefit from accepting as guidelines the emotional cues our dreams give us. If we learn to listen to our dreams from an emotional standpoint, we can garner much information to effectively guide us every day. It only makes sense for women to withdraw into a private retreat space when their hormones are preparing the way for emotional pointers on a dream map.

Most dreamers are aware of the transcendent quality of shamanic dreams or "guidance dreams." Unlike "processing dreams," which simply rehash our experiences to better integrate them, guidance dreams represent a different reality from ordinary reality, bringing the dreamer into a more revered place where spiritual guidance is more meaningful. Some dreams seem to be actual experiences. If one accepts the premise that both waking and sleeping experiences are authentic, this is true. If real experiences elicit feelings and guide one's actions, which I believe they do, transcendent dream experiences are as real as our everyday reality. We simply don't share that reality with others in the same way that we participate in the consensual reality of everyday life.

To a dreamer, dreams can help shape the way she or he views the world. If we follow the symbols of dreams and glean their meaning, dreams can make as much sense, if not more, than our waking experiences. If one takes the approach that dreams mirror insight and personal growth, paying attention to one's dreams is exceptionally important and could be one of the most important elements of spiritual understanding.

No dream can be fully interpreted without the participation of the dreamer, for only she or he knows the "feeling state" of the dream. If we don't treat our dreams with respect by trying to remember and act upon their guidance, their importance and their impact are wasted. Without listening to intuitive guidance, we simply move through the motions of living without understanding the meaning of the choices we make. If we honor our dreams and incorporate the spiritual guidance that comes through them, our lives can be greatly enhanced.

Many spiritual traditions teach that the reality we accept as the truth is only a dream of a higher reality. Some say our ordinary lives are a waking dream. We are the co-creators of a consensus reality through this waking dream. Einstein taught that all material things come from energy, and quantum physics confirms this understanding. Energy produces our thoughts and our dreams. Dreaming produces the guidance and the map to follow in our daily life. We just have to do one thing at a time, listen to our hearts, and dream our way to where we want to be. If we want to improve our lives and bring healing to our world, listening to our dreams in our waking life is paramount.

The divine feminine is trying to tell us that we have more power to co-create than we realize. Nature's timing for retreat enables us to be more emotionally open to receiving dream guidance that may be used to help others and ourselves. We may hear the guidance we need to correct imbalances in our lives, create solutions to challenges, and bring greater harmony into our families and our world.

10
Creativity Cycles

✧

WOULDN'T IT BE WONDERFUL if everyone recognized and could access opportunities to be creative and regenerative in their lives? For women, there is a biological four-step process that applies to creating new life or new ideas—purify, listen and incubate, create, and bloom. We can see this process at work in the creation of a child. In a woman's menstrual cycle, every month, old blood is released and fresh blood begins to build a new environment in preparation for the child. The special state of incubation called pregnancy allows the seed to germinate, to whisper to us in the dark of our wombs, to kick and move as we feel new life beginning to grow. The creative process peaks at the magical moment of birth. While we watch the being to whom we have given life grow and bloom, we continue to participate in the process of creation by offering a nurturing, supportive environment full of guidance to that child.

All women seeking to create new ideas, projects, and circumstances may use this creative process. The same creative process is available to men as well, although men's biological guidance has never been studied to help men understand the importance of honoring cycles of creativity. Nevertheless, I am certain men have cycles of creativity, and perhaps the steps of the creative process are not so very different for them.

EVERYDAY CREATIVITY

We can apply the above formula—purify, listen and incubate, create, and bloom—to create anything in our lives. Because of our biology and physiology, women are models of creation, yet our own culture treats the creative process lightly unless it involves giving birth, or the generation of an acclaimed work of art or literary achievement. Daily living involves creativity, too, yet daily living is rarely referred to as "art." To my mind that's wrong. There is an art to living that involves some stage of creativity in every moment. We should be aware that we are birthing our lives through our attitudes and our actions, and it is by understanding the process deeply that we can make positive and lasting changes in our lives.

For years psychologists have studied creativity. Psychologist Stanley Krippner defined creativity as any act, idea, or product that creates changes in an existing domain, or that transforms parts of an existing domain into a new one.[1] Psychologist and art therapist W. E. Anderson defined creativity as the ability to deal adequately and originally with a new situation or to deal innovatively with an old one.[2] Psychologist and M.D. Ruth Richards said that creativity encompasses divergent and fluid thinking, free association, and transformational abilities.[3] In *The Courage to Create* American existential psychologist Rollo May stated that true creators are those who give birth to some new reality.[4] In a personal conversation, Emilie Conrad provided my favorite definition of creativity, saying, "It is the emerging unexpected, the opposite of control and predictability. The creative consciousness is always listening in between; it is not a focused awareness; it is an omni-directional awareness." None of these definitions support the idea that creativity is the exclusive domain of specially gifted artists. These definitions tell us that creativity is something of which we are all capable. In fact, it is our divine right, and it is necessary for life.

The wonderful work of creativity maven Ruth Richards validates everyday creativity. She claims that creativity is valuable as a part of everyday life, explaining that everyday creativity is a fundamental survival need. She has defined creativity as doing something new in the course of one's activity at work or leisure. Richards has suggested that we must first embrace ourselves to embrace the kind of creativity that provides ultimate uniqueness along with ultimate interconnectedness. The ability to be creative is a core property of all living beings and a key aspect of mental health.[5]

In *Eminent Creativity, Everyday Creativity, and Health,* Richards lists seven important points to consider about the necessity of creativity in our lives. Creativity:

- Is not an optional extra for certain people, but rather is an essential capability for survival and ongoing development.
- Is not limited to special areas such as the arts, but rather can be found in all parts of life.
- Is not merely a light and pleasant diversion, but rather is a vital enterprise involving deep commitment, concentration, risk taking, and sometimes, personal transformation.
- Although sometimes unsettling, creativity is not fundamentally an enterprise that unsettles and evokes pathology, but rather is one that can open, integrate, and heal.
- Is not an endeavor focused only on end products, but rather involves a healthy way of approaching life, which connects us more meaningfully to our world, whether we are actively creating or appreciating the creativity of others.
- Is not an activity set apart from us, but rather is an activity that reaches deep into mind, body, and spirit and can help heal us, revealing a profound mind-body-connection we are only beginning to understand.
- Is not a neutral or safe activity that risks little, but rather can be a potentially dangerous enterprise offering disruption and change—including personal reorganization and potential threats to society's status quo. Against these forces of changes may be

arrayed powerful obstacles, internal and external, conscious and unconscious. But we cannot address them unless we know why our creativity may be eclipsed and hidden to begin with.[6]

Creativity is born from either a place of joy and a desire to add beauty and harmony to life, or from a place of inward discontent that knows change is necessary, or possibly both. Whatever is happening, when a person moves toward creativity, she or he is involved in listening. Without listening to what needs to change or to what is asking to be created, creativity does not happen. Creativity is intimately linked to listening to the whisper of something larger than ourselves, something that plants the idea within us and guides our thoughts and actions to bring the idea into reality—the voice of the divine feminine.

A person involved with creating beauty feels joy—a feeling connected with higher consciousness and the experience of honoring one's own potential. In other words, each of us holds the potential to connect to the divine feminine, to our own divinity, and to be creative on a daily basis. We are thereby able to heighten our own moods to enhance our lives. I have found that there is joy in any creation because it either adds something to the world or it relieves us from a place of intolerable stagnation. Without creativity in our lives, we become increasingly depressed, or we simply die.

One reason so many people disallow their own creativity is that they are uncomfortable claiming their own divinity. Unfortunately, Christianity and other fundamental religions have taught us that God is the only Creator. We have disassociated ourselves from understanding that we are all divine, and that we all have the ability to be creative. The divine feminine reminds us that we are part of a larger divinity, and therefore are co-creators. If we have trouble believing that we are divine, we will also have trouble believing that we have the power to create, or that what we do is creative. Accepting a smaller version of ourselves does not allow us to be the powerful co-creators that we actually are. Further, we give away our power when we claim that only someone smarter and more talented, or something greater than ourselves can create. We are naturally connected to the divine feminine; when we acknowledge this connection, she reminds us that every moment holds creative potential.

Creativity is a process available to all people at some level in everyday life, simply because the creative consciousness is always listening for the unexpected. It involves a certain willingness to be open and to take risks. It requires a certain freedom to listen for guidance or inspiration. It involves a willingness to let go of being governed by the usual standards of thought and action. If it is innovative, beautiful, and outside the norm, making a meal for one's family can be more creative than making a piece of art.

A newfound creative solution to a long-standing relationship problem can bring unanticipated harmony into everyday living. The more we listen to what needs to change, accept that we have the power to make changes, and act on the divine feminine's inspiration, the more we honor who we are as spiritual humans.

It is also useful to realize that most often our ability to experience things in new and creative ways comes through the body rather than through the mind. It is the body that actually records and reflects changes and acts on impulses and inspiration. The body conveys to the mind the understanding of new experiences, while the mind translates the experience into words so that we may communicate those experiences to others. Our bodies also hold unresolved trauma that the mind may not yet have comprehended. Because women can understand the creative process, given that they express it in the act of giving birth, they can teach others by example how to honor creative cycles.

A POWERFUL, CREATIVE TIME

To create, a period of preparation is necessary, whether it is the nine months required to incubate a child, or quiet time to incubate a new idea or project. A retreat where one withdraws from daily affairs for a reasonable time encourages listening to the divine feminine as she seeds inspiration into our consciousness. Without time to listen, there is very little space for new ideas to arrive. Often women who are having trouble conceiving have simply ignored this simple step—they are trying to fit getting pregnant into an already packed life. When we make space to be spontaneous, free, open to experience, and able to live more vividly in the moment (as opposed to the past or the future), we become more resilient. We are more consciously aware, and more appreciative of our fundamental interdependence, as well as the effects we have on each other and on the world.

Ruth Richards suggests that we should consider creativity as important to us as water, air, or food. It involves the give-and-take of all that we experience with each other and our surroundings. If we do not create a time and space to integrate the myriad energies that affect us daily, we can stifle the voice of the divine feminine. We also become numb to recognizing, understanding, or taking responsibility for how our own thoughts and actions affect others.

The blood changes that women experience give them a bodily awareness of the creative process. For women, menstruation is the first "mystery" associated with blood. Conception is second, and pregnancy is third. All are related to creativity. Menstrual bleeding relates to the cleansing and repairing phase, conception is the phase of divine inspiration, and pregnancy involves producing the product of that inspiration.

The Kolish Indians believe that enlightened wisdom stems from the body awareness that a young girl experiences during her first menses. Sharing the understanding of this process can help others realize what is necessary to manifest more ideas, greater problem solving abilities, or new thoughts, as well as how to creatively take the initiative to produce new projects or finish old ones.

Myths from many Earth-based societies claim that the time of women's bleeding is a powerful time for creativity. One of the foremost scholars of cultural myths Joseph Campbell (a man with a clear connection to the divine feminine) pointed out that one function of myths is to put one's way of life in harmony with nature. He spent his entire life studying worldwide myths and how those myths affected people's choices in daily living.

The myths of our current culture seem to separate us from nature. How have we allowed our myths to define who we are? We live with an imbalance that we intrinsically know is wrong. Our myths have given our children a legacy of confusion. Our children grow up in a culture that defines its members with desperately out of balance gender-specific roles that place masculine attributes above feminine attributes. The result of this "training" is that girls try to act like boys to be more accepted and boys ignore any aspects of the feminine that could contribute to their being more balanced individuals. Such divided, linear, and regimented thinking causes our children to continually strive for an imagined future via a science called progress, while ignoring possibilities that may be whispered in dreams or otherwise be derived from the imagination.

A clear example of balancing one's life with nature is evident in women's biological urges to slow down and be quiet during the time they are losing blood. Nature-based myths that require treating the fertility cycle as a sacred reality that holds the power to open our own creativity are quite valuable. Existential psychologist Rollo May, another man deeply in touch with the divine feminine, pointed out almost five decades ago that we should be able to retire from a world that influences us too much and be quiet to let solitude work for us and through us. We seem to have lost touch with this wisdom. Women's natural biological cycle is a key for all humans to listen to the timing of our own bodies and to accept the creative spark of life. Acknowledging the divine feminine keeps our own divine spark of creative potential alive. Cardiologist Ari Goldberger discovered that the healthy heartbeat is not regular and rhythmic, but contains chaotic irregularities that actually determine the organ's health and the individual's survival.[7] We must remember that life is change, and change is always involved in creativity. If we allow ourselves to be non-changing (or stuck), we die.

Women have always had a special time nature sets aside to expel the old and make room for the new. Men have a more challenging time designing retreat time for their own clearing and creative process. However, men can create their own retreat times by going camping either alone or with other men who have a similar purpose. The ManKind Project, MenSpeak, and A Circle of Men are examples of groups that encourage men to retreat together to regain the balance and harmony that they have lost in society's warped value system. We all need to honor times to slow down, listen, and wait. The divine feminine brings inspiration when we are just *being* rather than when we are focused on *doing*. When we wait before acting, our actions are accomplished more efficiently and more quickly because we have respected the pause in the creativity cycle. When we honor our own natural timing and become examples to others, everyone benefits from participating in the rhythms of life.

FORCES ACTING AGAINST OUR ABILITY TO BE CREATIVE

While hundreds of researchers have looked at what causes eminent creativity (that which produces extraordinary pieces of art or brilliant ideas) and everyday creativity (that which produces the art of living), no one is acknowledging that creativity has lessened in modern cultures. Even in school, science and progress are valued more than teaching our children the art of living. One of the greatest downsides of a patriarchal culture is that it separates us from our connection to nature, from the voice of the divine feminine, from our own divinity, and from our own innate creativity. When the Judeo-Christian patriarchal culture changed the structure of our belief systems, we lost much of our creative potential as humans. Fundamental religions have taken creativity away from the divine feminine and assigned it to a male god. When women's cycles were dismissed, dishonored, and disempowered, what women have to teach about creatively cycling through life in accord with nature was silenced.

By living the male model of progressive thinking and action, our lives have become hurried and harried. We perceive that we do not have time to slow down to smell the roses, to listen to the still small voice of our intuition or our spiritual guidance, or to connect with another person or an animal in a meaningful way—at least for any length of time. Human connection has been downsized to stealing a few hours to have lunch with a friend, a quick sexual encounter, or sadly, sending a catch-up email. Linear, progressive thought and value systems that focus on speed, constant achievement, and advancement have left little time for listening to and honoring our innate creativity. The creativity cycle has been dashed through the pressure of crunching time to get more done. It has been shut down by beliefs that there is only one Creator (God as Creator) who endowed only certain special individuals with the ability to create.

No one can define for another what is creative. The essence of creativity involves doing something that is out of the norm. Creativity arises out of spontaneity and cannot be bound by standard definitions. Any spontaneous action that brings something new and different can be creative. Results of such actions can include new recipes, new ideas about work projects, or sudden resolutions to long-standing problems.

Our creativity has been limited because of our separation from nature and our egotistic self-centeredness as humans. We are not the best of God's creations, nor are we necessarily highest on the chain of intellect, compassion, or interest in our environment. Look at the intelligence in dolphins, the compassion in whale communities, and the unconditional love in dogs to see how we are lacking. We are, perhaps the species with the largest ego and the strongest desire to control others. Humanity seems to be moving increasingly in the direction of separating ourselves from the rest of nature. Technological advances speed us up and simultaneously reinforce values of separation that will ultimately destroy us if we don't remember who we are and our connection to everything in the universe. The more we separate ourselves from nature, treating our precious lives merely as a daily grind to "get things done," the more we become lifeless robots. We must create to be fully alive. Mahatma Gandhi reminded us all that there is more to life than increasing its speed.

Slowing down and learning to listen are lost arts on the road to living a more creative life. Let me ask you these questions: Can you slow down? Can you change your values to allow time to listen? Can you accept that you are a divine part of nature? Can you create through your thoughts, your ideas, your spontaneous insights, and your intuition? Of course, you can! The real question is, will you make that choice? If you can, you will be making space for the divine feminine's inspiration and intuition to guide you. We must honor our biological and creative nature, and we must return to recognizing that we are part of nature, not her governors. Please, readers, consider what I am saying. Please allow time to really absorb the possibilities of being in the world in another way, a way that allows space for previously unthought-of ideas and spontaneous actions of all kinds to arise. Space is the mother of creativity. Allow space in your life, and your creativity will naturally increase.

As I move more and more slowly, creating space, what I am aware of in my own body reflects the dropping away of patterns and structures of who I used to be and how I *was* in the world. I am now creating a more fluid version of myself, one that is capable of flowing with the energies of the present, capable of listening to the guidance of the divine feminine, and capable of re-creating myself in new ways, moment-by-moment. I experience silence as moving waves—ripples of newness and possibility—as I ride the waves of my ever-evolving self.

11

Menopause Magic and Andropause Awakening

THE DUAL CHANGING NATURE of being female brings a poignant understanding that life is not only full of change, but that life *is* change. To live is to experience countless changes on a daily basis. That said, women experience even more changes within them in their monthly menstrual cycles. Menopause moves women into another stage of change, a stage that is quite beautiful when it is accepted as a coming into the full blossoming of wisdom, rather than lamenting it as the end of youth. In *Women's Bodies, Women's Wisdom,* Christiane Northrup, M.D., a pioneer in the field of women's health, defines menopause as an exciting developmental stage that holds enormous promise for transforming and healing bodies, minds, and spirits at the deepest levels when participated in consciously.[1]

Menopause is a time when women may listen more deeply to their intuition. Men have their own changes to allow deeper listening, even though these cycles, for the most part, have been ignored or disregarded. Men produce the exact same hormones that women do, but in different amounts. And with age, men's hormonal balance shifts, often resulting in weight gain, loss of energy or stamina, and a loss of interest or joy in living. As we have mentioned earlier, the timing of this hormonal change in men is called andropause.

Due to the fact that men's hormones are steady and constant for most of their lives, these sudden shifts in hormones can precipitate an unexpected emotional response to the changes they are experiencing in their physical bodies. Often termed a *midlife crisis,* the time of hormonal change in men is culturally viewed from a psychological viewpoint only. Yet changing hormonal levels affect every aspect of being male, just as hormonal changes affect women. In *Adrenaline Dominance,* Michael Platt, M.D., a specialist in natural hormone replacement, points out that unaddressed hormonal changes, such as long-term increased adrenaline, can lead to the physical and mental imbalances that manifest as disease.[2] In men, these imbalances can include coronary artery disease, prostate cancer, osteoporosis, and Alzheimer's disease. Despondency and depression often accompany these hormonal changes.

As with women, if men have not listened to their own inner guidance along the way, they may experience a tremendous process of grieving for what they have not achieved or anger about circumstances they have not changed. Hormonal shifts encourage honoring of where we have been and where we are now, and the extreme changes of both andropause and menopause require a reexamination of our emotional, mental, and physical bodies to achieve health and wholeness. Both andropause and menopause are times of life review and rebalancing in order to step into the fullness of who we are. The hormonal shifts occurring as we approach our wisdom years may just be the voice of the divine feminine calling us to return to a state of balance.

ANDROPAUSE: THE MALE EQUIVALENT OF MENOPAUSE?

Andropause, the time when a man's hormones shift as he loses testosterone, has been addressed even less than menopause because hormonal changes on a regular basis are much less evident in men than in women.

Women's cycles are clearly marked by hormonal swings that can be witnessed through the presence of a monthly release of blood. Men have no such outer symptom to suggest that their cycles are worthy of being studied. A man who suddenly feels grief or other emotions at the changes he is undergoing has no guidelines to show him how to move into the next valuable stage of his life. Our society simply does not honor wisdom that can naturally arise through the process of change brought about by aging. The emotional problems women and men have with menopause and andropause respectively are culturally induced. Unlike women, men have not been afforded even the idea that they should retreat to examine their inner lives. If a person has not listened to or acted on the urgings for change that are presented throughout his or her life, those urges build until an untenable necessity for change comes screaming forth as he or she approaches andropause or menopause.

Such a person may suddenly become tired of placing everyone else first, finding that she is now compelled to listen to and act upon what her heart and her body have always wanted. Or he may suddenly leave all that is familiar, searching for something to fill the emptiness that arrives as a result of the inner voice having been ignored. The urgings come forth like birth pains, and they sometimes give birth to a new face in the mirror that even we ourselves may not initially recognize. A lifetime of menstrual cycles without honoring the importance of retreat or without listening to emotional signals for change has brought many women to the edges of a chaotic menopause, where the body rebels in a fury of hot flashes and unhappy mood swings. A lifetime of constancy with no room for inner work has brought many men to the point of reckless behavior while they seek the truth about who they really are.

In *The Wisdom of Menopause,* Christiane Northrup empowers hormonal wisdom saying, "Our hormones are giving us an opportunity to see, once and for all, what we need to change in order to live honestly, fully, joyfully, and healthfully in the second half of our lives."[3] The changes necessary for the second half of life come more gracefully and with less force if we have spent a lifetime of listening to the urgings for change every month. Purging what is not working, listening deeply for guidance, and making continual changes in harmony with nature paves the path to our elder years with ease rather than struggle.

Our cultural attachment to the Hollywood ideal of the perfection of youth provides an additional impediment to a smooth transition into menopause or andropause. It's partially our own fault that such judgments land so hard when we reach menopause or andropause, for most of us have spent a lifetime accepting cultural definitions of beauty and worth. It upsets me to see young women hiding their natural beauty behind the latest style of clothing or brand of lipstick or a young man trying to make his appearance match that of the latest Hollywood role model. It's even worse when older women and men who seem desperate to cling to their youth exhibit these behaviors. While there is nothing wrong with enjoying our bodies and enhancing them, the vision of our inner beauty has been lost to external standards of perfection. Many people of both genders have been tricked into believing that they must stay young and productive forever in order to be loved and valued.

Both andropause and menopause have been associated with reaching the end of our productive years. Men struggle with lack of creativity when they find themselves without a fulfilling project. Women mourn the loss of the ability to produce a child, even if they have never chosen to give birth! For those women who have given birth, many of these women struggle to redefine their worth when the kids leave home. It happens so frequently that our culture has given this situation a name—*empty nest syndrome*. The same picture often arises for men, who have spent a lifetime defining themselves by what they do. Retirement spells lack of productivity and ineffectiveness to these men. Both women and men fall into the cultural fear that once they are no longer young and productive, they will be cast aside as useless, leading meaningless lives.

CREATIVITY IS AN ONGOING PART OF LIFE

Creativity does not stop when we can no longer produce a child or when we no longer have a regular job. I have listened to many clients, who are approaching retirement or experiencing the hormonal swings that signify a large change, express fears of simply being tossed aside by society or by those they love. Only recently have menopausal women begun to understand and embrace the fact that menopause is a stage that not only holds wisdom, but can also be full of creativity, freedom from assigned duties, and joyful satisfaction. Older women now have the time to pass on their wisdom to younger women.

As women begin to discover the possibilities inherent in a creative life in their later years, they can share this vision with elder men who may be struggling to understand their own worth in the absence of meaningful professional work. The divine feminine is calling us to change our views of who we are. Progressive patriarchal cultures abhor unpredictability and change, only valuing linear improvements in the status quo. Yet it is unpredictability and change that infuse us with life and allow for creativity. Many of us have spent our entire lives either defending unpredictable changes within us or feeling like victims of external changes around us. How many times have you heard your mate or friend say with exasperation, "But I thought you wanted . . . ?" If you are a man reading this, try to remember that women themselves have become confused by the patriarchy's attempt to dismiss or control the natural changes they experience.

If you are a woman reading this, you need to remember that it is not men's fault that they are confused by our continually changing choices and attitudes. It is ours. It is our responsibility to explore and understand our own needs for change, and then to share that understanding with our partners. Simply being changeable without explanation can appear to be irresponsible and fickle, and changing without apparent reason can cause undue stress and confusion in others.

Very few women have examined or tried to explain their dual ways of being in the world, an existence that requires different responses at different times. Instead, women have offered surface explanations, defended themselves, or struggled to be more constant, whether it was appropriate or not. By the time menopause arrives, most women have felt a compelling pressure to at least attempt to be constant, or barring that, to hide the effects of their cyclical needs and make the best of the changes that do occur. Changes that come in a woman's cycle are not linear and progressive. They are spiraling, creative, life-affirming, and often surprisingly unpredictable. When we seek to be constant and ignore the voice of the divine feminine within us, we not only hurt ourselves, we also lose the ability to model—for our male counterparts and society—the benefits of being flexible and changeable as circumstances dictate.

A CLOSER LOOK AT
ANDROPAUSE AND MENOPAUSE

While all men experience the biological phenomena of andropause, and all women experience the biological phenomena of menopause, it seems that only modern Western cultures consider either of these stages of life a medical event. Both menopause and andropause are considered hormonal imbalances. In America, menopause has been treated as a disease to be medicated. Andropause has either been ignored altogether or also defined as a pathological imbalance. Fortunately, enlightened medical doctors like Christiane Northrup and Michael Platt, who I have cited previously, are spending a great deal of energy educating people about the gifts of both menopause and andropause and offering medical support when needed, instead of medicating the problem away. As well, they are finally educating modern women and men about the value of our elder years. These gifted doctors deem both menopause and andropause to be opportunities for growth and renewal.

We are so deeply affected by both menopause and andropause for two reasons. The first has to do with cultural attitudes toward beauty, health, youth, and self-esteem. The second reason is that many of us have lived a lifetime of not honoring the processes of being a woman, or disallowing the divine feminine to speak through us as a man. In this we remain disconnected from our cyclical natures or our inner voices, and refuse to use duality and change to further our growth.

Be that as it may, just when we become accustomed to monthly changes (as women) or daily routines (as men), suddenly they are over. Or maybe not so suddenly. Maybe menopause or andropause creeps up on us, making us question who we are as our bodies move into unfamiliar territory and our emotions come to the surface, like a top that has been wound too tight and then suddenly let go. We start to miss a few periods (women) or engage in some reckless behaviors (men). Or our periods (women) and our emotions (men and women) surprise us with their intensity. There is a huge surge reminding us of what it is to be a human being experiencing emotional and bodily changes. We may experience an increase in tears or anger. Everything may seem intense; things seem to matter in a way that has never been so important. Our partners, children, and friends may look at us differently, as if we are different people, asking where is that predictable person that I used to know? They may question who we are and we may even question that ourselves. We may be afraid something is wrong, but actually, this is the way it is meant to be. It is different, not wrong.

I have lived most of my life jumping in feetfirst, taking on projects that require me to learn as I go. For instance, I clean a closet by pulling everything out into the middle of the floor. Ironically, my body apparently understood this approach, because I also jumped into menopause. I went from having regular monthly cycles to a complete cessation of bleeding within the space of two months. The monthly flow was replaced with deep sadness, hot flashes that left me soaking wet with limp, soggy clothes clinging to my body, and torrents of tears streaming down my cheeks. Because I had only just started to honor my cycles before they ended, unresolved issues came out with abandon. I was angry at things I thought I had forgotten about years ago.

The truth is that I had dismissed them when they had disturbed me, and unresolved, they were lying in wait in my body, ready to explode emotionally in response to the hormonal changes of menopause. While this is probably an extreme example of change, there is likely some familiarity to the emotional and physical pattern that comes to the forefront when the inner voice has never or rarely been acknowledged and the body has been forced into unnatural rhythms. I suspect both men and women reading this story can relate to the compelling urge to discover who you are when such physical and emotional states demand your full attention.

Do menopause and andropause have to be so uncomfortable? I don't think so. Our cultural assumptions about these transitional times, coupled with our throwaway attitudes and societal beliefs that we are only desirable when we are young and productive, predispose us to expectations that the change of life (menopause or andropause) will bring nothing but loss. As long as a man has the choice to work, he retains his social value. A woman's social value may be tied to a career or to being a mother. Once those roles are finished, both men and women may feel lost and bewildered. The belief that the change of life brings loss still lurks in the subconscious of many of us, and the end of fertility or productivity signals a decline in self-esteem. Psychological belief systems and attitudes influence the intensity of menopausal and andropausal symptoms. And seeing this change of life as a negative event has contributed to difficult transitions in modern cultures.

MENOPAUSE AND ANDROPAUSE ARE OPPORTUNITIES IN DISGUISE

Menopause and andropause point to the momentous significance of stepping fully into being all that we are. It is at this point that both women and men frequently eliminate everything that is not working in their lives and begin to share with others what they have learned along the way. If we have done our work, menopause and andropause offer a time of blossoming, as we become all that we can be and step forward to share our wisdom with others. We can wake from the sleepy forgetfulness that has compelled so many to mourn their cycles rather than celebrate them. We can look back and be glad. We can begin to rearrange the cultural attitudes that have inhibited us, demonstrating the power of using our intuition, cooperation, and unconditional love. We no longer have to accept the patriarchal beliefs that have defined who we are as women or as men.

Once we rearrange our own views and dismiss erroneous beliefs about who we are, we can help to create, from a place of inner acceptance, contentment, and personal power, different paths for our daughters and our sons. It is only when we have acquired such knowing and acceptance of ourselves and put away childish competitions or desires to be younger again that we can begin to shine the light of peace and love into the world. Each cycle we have experienced has culminated in this moment. We either unleash the fury of previously unheeded impulses for change in a deluge of physical and emotional distress, or we fully understand the beauty of being who we are in this and every cycle of life. Perhaps our whole lives have led up to the moment we cross into menopause or andropause, like a bud opening to full flower. This is a magical time when wisdom flows instead of blood, when we can offer perspective rather than productivity.

Menopause and andropause are indeed opportunities. They are the times of emptying and refilling—times of change, so smile at the river of fire that courses through you as you come into a new place of balance. Be willing to take your sweater on and off a few times as your inner thermostat regulates to your new climate. Don't walk around looking for productive projects to do. Instead, learn to relish quiet listening and the discovery of a slower pace. Reintroduce yourself to your natural environment and make friends with the wind, the sun, the rain, and the trees. Gaze at the moon and watch the stars. Listen to the greater calling as the divine feminine moves more fully into your heart. If you have never listened to your body, start now. Listen to the messages in your emotions. If you have never experienced a sacred time to cleanse what is not working and create new harmony in your life, do so now.

Once you have listened to what your body needs, worked with your shadows, and healed your heart, you will be ready to use your emotional guidance to speak out against injustice. Be a champion for the Earth. Share what you know about the extraordinary blessings of listening to the divine feminine and following nature's guidance, helping others to find their own way back into balance. Above all, honor who you are and that you have done the very best you knew how to do or had the courage to do in any given moment. If you made mistakes or poor choices, seek an understanding about what caused you to make those choices and learn more about yourself. We learn from the experiences where, perhaps, we did not do all that was possible. Ask yourself what it would take to have more courage to change things in your life, and then summon that courage.

This may be the point where some of us take a long look at the past, grieving certain choices, or even wishing for things to be different. We cannot change the past, but we can change the effects of the past by doing things differently now and moment by moment. This way of being conscious in the present helps us to create a future that better matches our dreams. To be happy it is imperative that we learn to accept what is with dignity and grace, that we stand up for our rights and our needs, that we do not make poor choices through a desire to be loved, that we do not fold in the face of conflict, that we live from authenticity and integrity, and that our choices honor the highest good for all.

The duality of extremes in cyclic separation and return are no longer necessary in my life in the way they once were. Perhaps it's because I passed into menopause with a greater understanding of how to listen, or perhaps it's more related to my ongoing understanding of the presence of duality in everyday life. Whatever the reason, when my heart-mate and I do choose to spend time alone, our experience holds more unity than separateness; our times of togetherness are closer, richer, and deeper on all levels than I ever imagined possible. I am blissfully blessed in my relationship, and whatever we are experiencing together or separately is just right for that moment. We are cycling together in life and through life. I suggest that a real honoring of our cyclic nature may automatically move all of us toward a cosmic spiral of greater unity and greater connection.

Remember that there is wonder in being someone who has attained the wisdom of listening to one's heart and one's body. This is a time to demonstrate the power of unconditional love and your divine right to say no or yes as your heart guides you. This is a time to nurture new ideas and new understandings about life. It is also the time to help our daughters and our sons understand that by listening to the voice of the divine feminine and aligning themselves with the cycles of nature, they hold the power to change the world.

12

The Water We Are

THE DIVINE FEMININE calls us to remember that we are largely water and, as such, we carry the same possibilities for flowing and responding to each person, or energy, that we encounter, changing ourselves as circumstances require, moment by moment.

To more fully explore this, let's look at the connection between water and life. Science has proven that life originated in the sea. Science has also shown chemical similarities between ocean water and blood, both made of salt and water. The human fetus is surrounded by sea-like amniotic fluid. As embryos, humans are 97 percent water. At birth, our water can be measured at 78 percent; by adulthood, it's approximately 60 percent.

Water in women flows out in rhythms with the moon in the form of blood, as we shed what our bodies no longer need. The wet blood from a woman's body is the moisture that brings forth life. The female body presents a living example of the connection between water and life. Ethnographic studies have shown that many Earth-based cultures throughout the world have compared the life-giving blood of women to the life-giving water of Mother Earth. Myths from earlier times often refer to water as the blood of the Earth. In Mesopotamia, caves, streams, and the sources of rivers were compared to the vagina of a woman. Indeed, in Babylonia, the term *pu* meant both "source of a river" and "vagina." Sumerians used the word *buru* to mean both "river" and "vagina." We are made of water, and understanding that makeup helps us to relate to life with a greater sense of flow.

Water, in its liquid state, always flows. In *Experimenting with Water,* science teacher and author Robert Gardner breaks apart the exact parameters of water in the human body with these percentages:[1]

▲ Blood is 90% water;
▲ The brain holds 85% water;
▲ Muscles hold 75% water;
▲ The liver is 66% water;
▲ The living cells hold 60%;
▲ Bone is 22% water;
▲ The space between cells consists of 25% water;
▲ Blood plasma holds up to 95% water;
▲ Cavities of organs such as eyes and lubricant for joints are 5% water.

Gardner's statistics give a factual representation of just how important water is to human life, although clearly the amounts vary from person to person. When we understand the human connection of life to water, we have a deeper respect for the water of the planet and the water that we are. William Marks, an expert on water and the author of *The Holy Order of Water,* encapsulates the importance of water, saying that "If life did begin in the sea, then we are alive only because we carry our own sea within us."[2]

To signify the importance of water, Theodor Schwenk, anthroposophist, engineer, pioneering water researcher, and author of the book *Sensitive Chaos,* interchanged the words *water* and *life.* As I read Schwenk's work, I noticed continual similarities to the waters of life and the divine feminine consciousness. Below are Schwenk's observations with my own comments italicized in brackets:

Life works chiefly as a synthesizer, forming wholes that are greater than the sum of all their parts. [*The divine feminine helps us to balance many small things, different parts of life, in order to have a better-ordered total.*] Water moves rhythmically, not, however in a mechanically measured beat. Life is always a little bit eccentric. Water is responsive to cosmic rhythms, indeed, entirely governed by them. [*Women display this pattern through monthly cycles.*] Therefore, life flows in cycles rather than in straight-lines or in a mechanical way. [*Following the divine feminine is following the guidance of our bodies, rather than governing our lives through a calendar or clock.*] Water always leaves itself free space for maneuvering. [*The divine feminine encourages us to remember that nothing is definite because change is always a possibility.*] Life never submits to exact calculations. [*The divine feminine helps us to change our minds according to circumstances as they arise.*] Life moves in cycles wherein metamorphoses and heightenings take place. It is attuned to the cosmos [*life's rhythms and water's rhythms*] and to endlessness in time and space. [*When one is acting from the divine feminine, it is possible to be more aware of everything around you simultaneously.*] In every area, water assumes the role of mediator. [*The divine feminine continually encourages us to be peacemakers in the world.*][3]

THE IMPORTANCE OF FLUIDITY

The consciousness that is present in water lives within all of us, both women and men, although it may be more apparent in women because of women's cycles. We are all made of water, and we all have the possibility of behaving more like the water we are in our everyday lives. Biological cycles make it more natural for women to honor these traits, but men also have the ability to be more like water when they allow the divine feminine to work through them to bring flexibility, cooperation, and willingness to see others' viewpoints. When we choose to behave like water, all of us can move rhythmically, flowing with circumstances as they occur. All of us can tune in to Earth's rhythms and honor them, rather than trying to control nature or mechanize our lives through a progressive, linear mode of living. All of us can be less rigid and allow ourselves the freedom of changing our minds according to changing situations.

I asked Cullen how he views women as being like water. His response was that women, like water, often start to go one way and then quite unpredictably they go another. For the more linear gender, this quality must at times be quite exasperating, even if they carry those inclinations from the divine feminine within themselves, too.

Any time we change directions without warning, we can cause chaos around us. A sudden change of lanes when driving because we change our mind can be dangerous to all. Thus, it is the responsibility of each of us to be conscious of the effect we have on others when we make sudden changes. Or, if we want our changeability to be respected, we must ourselves become clear in our intentions and constant in following them through. Feminine changeability is about having a dual nature that follows nature's guidance as different circumstances arise. It is not about changing our mind midstream and confusing others. It is not about being wishy-washy about what we think, feel, or need.

If we women want to help our male counterparts become more flexible and changeable, then we ourselves must learn to be constant when appropriate. The application of both elements is balanced and wise. Ignoring the importance of biological timing has led to imbalanced states in both women and men; many men have become too definite, perhaps even rigid in their beliefs or approach to life. Many women have become too changeable, often uncertain and perhaps at times even unreliable. The divine feminine is offering us the chance to bring balance back into our lives, teaching us to choose change or constancy according to circumstances. The divine feminine flows like water.

NAVIGATING LIFE LIKE A RIVER

When I think of the many qualities of water, I'm amazed at how often those of us who are aware of the divine feminine presence within us emulate those same qualities as we navigate our lives. The English language is full of colorful phrases reflecting the changing properties of water. We use these water-based phrases to describe our human interactions. Consider these:

▾ Her heart was cold as ice;
▾ His heart melted;
▾ He was so angry you could see steam coming from his ears;
▾ She flowed from one task to another.

Each of these phrases invokes a quality of water to express the particular experience.

The divine feminine encourages us to be like water in our problem solving and to become aware of the power we carry in the way we meet obstacles. Think of a flowing river. When the water meets a rock, the water responds in one of several ways. Perhaps it can easily flow around the rock. If the surge of water (as in a flash flood) is strong enough, it might cause the rock to move. Or water can rise above the rock and flow over it. These fluid movements are familiar tools the divine feminine offers to help us handle challenging situations in life. When confronted with a seemingly insurmountable obstacle, the divine feminine encourages us to be the water we are and find a gentle solution. Those who are aware of the divine feminine in themselves are natural peacemakers, striving to find peaceful or cooperative solutions to obstacles when possible. Using tactics of antagonism or competition only causes more separation between us. The divine feminine helps us to understand how to make choices that allow others to be who they are and continue on their paths while we simply flow around them, following our own path. This way of interacting eliminates resistance and increases the flow of harmony.

I am troubled by how many women have adopted masculine models for dealing with conflict, rather than using the feminine, water-like model that is more natural to them. It seems that many women have lost their understanding that the divine feminine power of cooperation can be a greater force than aggressive or competitive masculine power. The reason for this loss of understanding stems from cultural, systemic devaluation of feminine attributes. It is a tragedy to see women model themselves after the gender that has ignored and suppressed them, emulating the very principles that have caused their suffering. On the other hand, it's a joy to see so many men waking up to the realization that the divine feminine is guiding them into more cooperative and intuitive ways of living.

ANDROGYNOUS WATER: AN ELEMENT OF UNITY

It could be said that water is androgynous, shaping itself according to the requirements of the moment. In our human evolution, we as water beings are also moving toward being androgynous (not genderless, but more oriented toward seeing the whole and shaping ourselves moment by moment as circumstances require). As androgynous beings, we incorporate both the divine feminine and the divine masculine within us, regardless of our gender. When we seek greater understanding and more harmonious views of life, we move away from the polarizations that have continually separated us.

This way of living can bring peace to the world. Women have an advantage in peacemaking endeavors, for women are whole-brain thinkers, joining right-brained creative thinking with left-brained analytical thinking through the corpus callosum. Therefore, women have two biological attributes (biological cycles is the other one) that can help lead us all through the maze of duality's polarized differences into a unified, balanced, and peaceful way of life.

Water is often used as an element of unity in ceremonies throughout the world. Native Americans unite physical life and spiritual life in sweat lodge ceremonies (Plains tribes) and river plunges (Cherokee). Christians sprinkle water on newborn babies or partially immerse them in water to unite their physical life with their spiritual souls. Immersion in the Jewish mikvah bath represents a change in a woman's spiritual status. Each of these ceremonies uses water as a symbol of life. Immersing oneself in water symbolizes a cleansing and reuniting with the flow of life. Women carry the most celebrated water ceremony of all within their own bodies: the ritual of monthly bleeding that announces the possibility of bringing forth a new life, for life is not possible without passing through water—the blood of a woman.

Even with all of this ceremonial use of water, we still suffer from appalling disrespect of both women and water in modern societies. The blood of Earth (our rivers and streams) and the blood of women have lost their sacred value. Both have been used as a commodity—polluted, blocked, or otherwise dammed to prevent the natural flow of change that both water and feminine principles represent. Those who cry for change are often blocked by cultural patterns and beliefs.

Feelings are related to water because they are fluid and changeable. Like water, feelings can nourish us or, if blocked, they can become harmful to us and to those around us. We often misuse the waters of our emotions in relationships with others. Knowing how to listen to our rising feelings in a timely manner is no different than knowing how to interact with the ocean's tides. Water and humans are both affected by gravitational pulls of the moon, and both respond to that pull. As we know, this tidal pull holds sway over our emotions. While women have emotional responses specific to their cyclic nature, they are not the only ones who can benefit by listening to what the emotions are trying to tell us. For too long men, in their culturally prescribed roles of being constant, dominant, and controlling, have curbed or internalized their own feelings or have succumbed to the pattern of emotional outbursts that occur when too many feelings have been suppressed for far too long.

It is through unblocked, unrepressed awareness that we can find the messages our emotions are trying to convey in order for us to make appropriate changes in ourselves and in our lives. Having a private place to work with our inner waters gives us the benefit of resolving issues without allowing our emotions to harm others. All emotions can guide us. Feelings of compassion, trust, and joy tell us that we are on the right path. Anger, grief, frustration, or jealousy point toward changes we need to make within ourselves. When the waters of emotion swell, clamoring to be recognized and acknowledged, and we examine their messages, we can choose to change ourselves or our situation, or we can choose to blame others for our misery. Continued repression of an emotion is no different than blocking a river. Eventually the river will overflow its banks, and the flood can be devastating.

Let me be clear: I am not a fan of histrionic expressions of emotion. I am not advocating that we should respond to every unsettling incident in our lives with an outburst of tears or a blast of angry words. I am proposing that through the sacred retreat process put forth in this book, we can all learn to listen to the messages of our emotions and act on their guidance. The gift of being in harmony with the tides of the ocean keeps us connected to nature in a special way, and it is our responsibility to honor that connection through our daily living, modeling it for others.

RESPECT AND UTILIZE THE RIVERS OF LIFE

When tears flow, there is movement, just as when a river flows. According to Cherokee tradition, it is a good practice to go to the water at the beginning and at the end of every day. With each visit, one asks the river to take from you what is not yours or what is not needed (anger, blame, resentment, grief) and to bring you what you do need (insight, inspiration, balance, kindness, compassion). The Cherokee understood that we can blend our own human water to the waters of Mother Earth and learn how to be more fluid in our lives. It may not be practical to find a river and immerse ourselves at the beginning and end of each day. But we certainly can mentally use the practice to purify our thoughts, quiet our minds, and open ourselves to inspiration and compassion for others.

Living our lives in a way that flows like water, spiraling toward higher consciousness, allows us to be more truly who we are and offers examples for our children about making appropriate choices. The analogy of being like a flowing river can help us to realize that we, too, can create an easier way of navigating life's challenges and difficulties. We are not meant to live in a way that promotes competition and conflict from the polar opposites of duality. Rather we are meant to see and value the varying aspects of dualistic experience as a way of offering a wider perspective of the whole and possibilities for greater unity. The divine feminine is calling us to marry the differences within ourselves and between each other through honoring sacred timing of all cycles of life. Respect and honorable treatment of our differences could be a model for changing the world.

The Anishinabek people call women the Keepers of the Water. As such, it is the responsibility of women to teach respect for the Spirit of Water, which gives life to everything else. Water as life-giver and woman as life-giver share a deep connection. It is the divine feminine that gives us the understanding of connection between water and life. It is the divine feminine that is calling us to protect and care for the water we are and the water of our planet. Those of us who recognize and are attuned to the divine feminine have a greater responsibility to demonstrate harmonious living through using all the gifts of being like water.

It is unnatural for water to remain still. The essential nature of water is movement, and by constantly moving, water serves to create, protect, energize, nourish, and sustain life. This movement can ultimately deliver possibilities, understanding, resolution, and peace. All humans are made of water, and like water, we can continually move toward creating conditions that are conducive to a balanced life if we choose. If we are made of water, which we certainly are, we must care for our inner waters and the inner waters of others, for we are all drops of the same ocean. If we pollute our waters with negative thoughts, those thoughts travel to the waters of others to pollute them as well. We are connected, and we need to recognize that, as water beings, we share a level of communication with every bit of water on the planet. This understanding can profoundly change our relationships. Caring for another's water is, quite simply, living in love.

In personal conversations with the late Emilie Conrad and in her pioneering book, *Life on Land*, Emilie shared her view of the connection of water to love. She wrote:

> In an amazing way, water also brings us the quality of love—a love that is beyond human possession, beyond altruism, perhaps a love that we are yet to realize. The movement of fluid within us is characterized by wave motion. These undulating wave motions become increasingly more subtle as every part of us begins to shimmer with the memory of our origin. The caresses of these fluid waves bring about an erotic, sensual, spiritual union—a cosmic return that words cannot even begin to describe.
>
> Wave motions represent not only our biological rapport with the universe; they rock us in a lush cradle. . . .
>
> It took me many years to recognize that the undulating fluid that I felt in my body is the movement of love. Looking back, it seems so obvious—that the undulating waves of primordial motion are the movements of love. Not emotional love but an encompassing *atmosphere* of love. A love that has its own destiny. Perhaps using humans as its messengers, this love is trying to land on Earth.[4]

Emilie's words reflect the call of the divine feminine in a profound and vital way. William Marks, author of the previously mentioned book, *The Holy Order of Water*, also speaks of the relationship between water and love, telling us that when two people fall in love, the water in every cell of their being resonates in harmony. Here is a man who clearly heard the divine feminine calling us to find ways to harmonize our differences. The cellular resonance of which Marks speaks is something that should be familiar to each of us. Perhaps women have an advantage in being able to feel this, since each woman feels the moon's pull on her internal waters from her first menstrual cycle. But each and every one of us can learn to pay attention to gravitational forces at a cellular level.

It's no surprise to experience cellular resonance of one's water when you connect with another human being, whether that is a child, a lover, or a good friend. We communicate water to water. (See the book that I coauthored with Cullen, *Conversations with Laarkmaa,* for a more thorough explanation of this phenomenon.) When one is in perfect resonance with another, the connection is simultaneously exhilarating and familiar. You flow toward the other person because your water feels resonance with the other person's water.

We may discover this resonance at varying levels in personal interactions, from feeling comfortable with a friend to complete and total immersion of oneself with a lover. I waited my whole life for my heartmate, who brought me instant understanding of the magnitude of intercellular resonance with the perfect mate. When I first hugged Cullen, I knew something was different and special about our connection. The water of my body stirred with a peaceful resonance. Unquestionably the water in his body was speaking to the water in my body through the rhythmic beating of our hearts. We learned about each other's hopes, dreams, and world view solely through the art of letter writing, yet my body remembered the rightness of that single first hug, and we continued to send and receive messages through our water, even when we were not physically together. After six and a half months of letter writing only, I once again heard Cullen's voice. In that moment, my heart burst forth in rainbow colors and flooded my entire essence with love. Soon after, we joined our lives together.

The resonance of love moves through us like water. When we recognize that all of life depends upon the health and balance of both water and the divine feminine, we can understand that we need to reinstate ways to honor them. A return to using principles of the divine feminine to guide our lives would benefit all of us, irrespective of gender. Our bodies, made of water, thrive on movement and flow. Like all bodies of water, when we utilize opportunities to cleanse, change, and flow, we allow the rivers within us to moisten the land upon which we live. Healthy rivers, in us or on Earth, support life. We are connected to each other and to everything on the planet through water.

13

Welcoming the Divine Feminine

THE TIME HAS NEVER been more critical for welcoming the divine feminine and returning to the wisdom of our natural cycles. Feminine consciousness resides within all of us, yet it has been suppressed. Linear thinking, a focus on continual progress, increasing speed, and the use of technology at the expense of honoring our environment in word and deed are causing further and further separation from nature, our source of life.

In ancient times, women were responsible for leading us toward balance so that harmony, peace, and health could prevail. As feminine values of cooperation have been dismissed and replaced with values of progress and competition, our world has become one of discord. The problem of imbalanced relationships, both personally and globally, has grown large enough to require our most urgent attention. It is now up to all of us, women and men alike, to return to core values of love and unity. We must make a great shift from the patriarchy back to the matriarchy. The call of the divine feminine is within us, whispering (and sometimes shouting), and the future of our species depends upon our listening and welcoming its presence by returning to natural cycles of balance, harmony, acceptance, and respect. It is connection that we need for our very survival, both as individuals and as part of a system of life on Earth.

Long before I skipped along the ocean shore as the tide flowed in and out, long before I felt my own tides coursing through my body every month, long before I studied natural cycles of life in school, I understood the presence of the divine feminine in nature. Yet as an impressionable child, I allowed the myths of modern culture to overpower my inner knowing.

If we do not like the effects of living by these cultural myths, we must recognize the underlying problems held within these myths and begin to change them—to rewrite the mythical instructions for living. Change of this magnitude requires relinquishing cherished beliefs about who we are and learning to trust our inner knowing instead. We must abandon the myths born out of or influenced by patriarchal ideas exemplified by the Christian Church. As we know, these myths have placed women in a subordinate position. The divine feminine power of Mother Mary has been dismissed as she has been pushed into a lesser role as mother of Christ, rather than a divine and powerful presence in her own right.

To extinguish any idea that the divine feminine could offer anything of value, Mary Magdalene, life mate and divine feminine partner to Christ, has been dismissed as well. In her case, she was deemed to be simply a sinner who was saved by Christ.

These views have worked their way into our subconscious, causing more and more separation as we have accepted existing myths that valued dominance. Instead, we might remember that we have the wisdom and the power to make our own choices. The divine feminine is urging us to shake off these erroneous beliefs and find our way back to the balance of love. To do this, we must begin to question everything we think, hear, feel, and know.

THREE WAYS TO RESTORE THE DIVINE FEMININE
TO OUR LIVES AND TO OUR WORLD

An important first task for returning to the balance of the divine feminine is to rewrite women's place in the world by honoring women as
beings who are blessed with one of nature's cycles every month. Ways
to do this include creating a sacred space for women to experience this
potent time, recognizing that an increased level of intuitive and dream
guidance occurs during cycles of quiet retreat, and slowing down and to
listen to what emerges from these sacred times.

Some specifics that may help you to change how you treat your
sacred cycles include:

▲ Decorating your retreat space in a way that feels and looks sacred
to you.

▲ Spending as much time as possible in retreat during menses.
Sleeping alone is wonderful, but you may also wish to spend days
in your sacred space as well.

▲ Paying close attention to what you feel.

▲ Paying attention to what you *think* about what you feel.

▲ Asking yourself if there is another way to view a situation.

▲ Journaling your feelings, thoughts, dreams, and ideas.

▲ Indulging your body with warmth and comfort (herbal teas
are great during retreat, as are hot water bottles and lots of
blankets).

▲ Asking others to provide food for you so that you can receive
while you are purging.

▲ Inviting your creativity to emerge by surrounding yourself with
colored pencils, crayons, paper, and/or other creative materials.

▲ Paying close attention to your dreams and listening for intuitive
guidance.

▲ Meditating through emptying your mind of *all* thoughts and
expectations.

▲ Releasing your "task list" and allowing yourself to respond spontaneously to life.

▲ Practicing gratitude for the gift of your life, your talents, your learning experiences, and for those whom you love.

A second task is to release men from the myth that requires them to unrelentingly push toward progress and a continued controlling of nature without enjoying space or time for their own cycles of rest or inner contemplation. This can be accomplished by understanding that there is a proper timing for everything, and we cannot push to make things happen faster than they naturally should. We must relinquish the belief that it is men's responsibility to fix all problems or organize the ways in which we approach all problems. It is this belief that has led to the erroneous idea that it is our right and our job to control the Earth and other creatures, rather than respecting the wisdom of the natural world and responsibly participating with it.

One way to change this belief system (and our accompanying behaviors) is to incorporate a period of contemplative or meditative experience in our everyday lives, rather than filling up each hour with as many tasks as possible. Through quiet meditation, the wisdom of our hearts can lead our brains to new and more imaginative ways of thinking and being in the world.

A third task is to set good examples for our daughters and our sons, teaching them the wonder and power of natural cycles and how to honor themselves, each other, and the gifts they have. It would behoove us to teach them about the creative principles of sexual exchange and how to appropriately deal with the strong currents of sexual energy they feel. Education that goes beyond the cultural dictates that posit that youth should abstain from sex, waiting until marriage to participate in it, is sorely needed. These old-paradigm rules do not address the reality of the sexual energy that young people feel coursing through them. A discussion of sexual energy might best be reframed as being a sacred opportunity to appropriately connect with another and with Source in a true experience of unity. To explain these things to our young we need to understand them ourselves.

The presence of the divine feminine has always governed rules for sexual connection. For thousands of years this was the sacred responsibility of women. It is now the sacred responsibility of both women and men, as the divine feminine guides us to consider the highest good for all when we sexually engage, urging us to connect only through love. Reclaiming responsibility to teach our daughters and our sons how to honor cycles of nature could correct much of what is out of balance between genders.

A beginning step might be to reexamine our thoughts about and treatment of women's cycles. Worldwide indigenous myths about menstruation, so different from our own, tell us that having a monthly cycle is not a curse, but rather a beautiful representation of how to live our lives within nature's flow. Some who are aware of these natural rhythms may feel ineffective in managing their lives according to the linear patriarchal guidelines of modern culture. Women may particularly feel awkward varying home or work routines according to where they are in their menstrual cycles. They want to do a good job and make a difference, but they often feel their natural inclinations are discounted as frivolous, irrelevant to material progress, or just plain wrong. Pregnancy and childbirth in America are often seen as an impediment to a career, while in other countries these parts of the creative cycle are valued, as they were by our ancestors. Workers (both women and men) in other countries are given months off to adapt to the changes in their lives because companies know that they will come back to work more balanced and ready to do their jobs.

THE NEED TO LIVE LIFE AT A HUMANE PACE

The real curse in Western patriarchal society is the unrealistic valuing of linear progress and constancy. Increased productivity and consistency in performance are not the only important values that should be promulgated in the workplace. Teaching our children to slow down enough to think through problems and use their intuitive and creative gifts can change the way we do business. We have taken the heart out of the workplace and encouraged workers to respond like the machines they use, without consideration for individual situations or sensitivities. Our youth do not know how to think or reply to any question or problem that is outside the box. They are encouraged to communicate using computers wherein all personal nuance of expression is lost. Everything is about speed, speed, speed. How often have you heard, "My computer says . . . " or "According to Google . . ." in response to a question you've asked in a store?

It's time for our youth to slow down and think through how best to find resolution of a problem and reward them for taking the time to do so. When an employee takes the time to feel what the customer must be experiencing or to figure out how to solve a problem, productivity and customer satisfaction are actually increased. Monitoring our habitual thoughts about our everyday lives is an excellent starting place for making this change. We can reeducate ourselves and our children about the benefits inherent in slowing down and taking the time to use our intuition and knowledge to solve problems and interact with others. Part of welcoming the divine feminine comes with welcoming these slower rhythms that are aligned with the natural rhythms of the Earth. There are many modern countries who know that allowing their employees adequate time away from work enhances worker creativity and productivity. Unfortunately, America is not one of them.

Just as women struggle with cultural attitudes against slowing down during menstruation, men also can feel judged for wanting to go for a walk in the forest or withdrawing into their own meditations when there is work to be done. In a personal conversation, Swedish journalist and CEO of Nordic Light Media, Erika Mikaelsson, told me that she believes many aware men are simply tired from accepting the responsibility of honoring the divine feminine within them when other men will not even acknowledge the need to do so. These men may find that they need to rest, repair, and prepare for the future, recognizing that it is now a time for women to once again step into power by leading from the position of the divine feminine—equally with men. It will take an honoring of natural cycles in both sexes to achieve this balance.

When we synchronize our lives with printed calendars and artificial rhythms ruled by electric lights, natural rhythms of rest and regeneration that follow nature's rhythm of day and night are denied. Our artificial man-made timing spurns the wisdom of the body. Because of this, times for our most precious inspirations are postponed until nights and weekends, when we may simply be too tired to do anything but collapse into an exhausted sleep. Changing our myths means changing how we think.

How can we move from such a weakened position to a position of power (not force)? We begin by talking about and then implementing other rules. Why not institute policies that support our taking time off from work for rest and regeneration; policies that are more balanced with the need to work? Why not give employees longer vacations, longer maternity and paternity leaves, less hours of work per day? Could our cultural priorities be realigned so that people are appropriately paid for teaching our children and creating beautiful art, rather than spending enormous sums on competitive sports and national defense? These are changes that we can make collectively if we decide that our modern myths of separation, competition, and control are simply not bringing us the peaceful and harmonious lives we deserve.

OTHER CULTURAL CONSTRUCTS
TO DECONSTRUCT

If our myths do not support a belief in our gifts and harmony with nature and each other, how can we change the cultural environment? We begin by taking time to think about what we believe, and to ask the question, "Is this really true?" We reexamine whether we really want to give our little boys toy guns. We protect our children from cultural ideas of violence that are in all the cartoons they watch. We take away computer games and teach our children to engage with each other to correct their retarded social skills. We stop supporting Little League and other competitive sports. We don't buy the bumper sticker that says, "My child is #1."

Another solution would be to teach our children about cooperation, and help them understand that it takes *everyone* to succeed. Rather than tolerating culturally assigned gender roles or accepting traditional viewpoints asserting our right to control nature, we can begin to see with a larger vision. If we realign our cultural world view so that we abandon the artificial speed of living and begin to live in flow with rhythms of the natural world, we can achieve enhanced harmony in our lives.

As a culture we have lost the awareness of differences between doing and being, and the appropriateness of right timing for both. *Doing* requires participating in life by taking action. *Being* requires slowing down (or withdrawing temporarily) to listen to one's intuition and guidance before acting. Anyone who is continually in a role of action will eventually find himself or herself caught in patterns of reaction and possibly even overreaction, if they do not allow space for clearing, introspection, intuition, guidance, and creative problem solving. Likewise, we are missing a general understanding of the natural flow between giving to others and nurturing ourselves. Nature is not static, and we are part of nature. We have seasons as well—times to be dormant and times to bloom.

All things that manifest in this world originate with a dream, a vision, a feeling, or a thought. Given this, participating in the creation of our reality by honoring cycles of deep listening increases our power. The potential for harmony within all relationships stems from this practice. It's our sacred responsibility to listen and bring creative ways of healing to the world, and to teach our children to be better listeners also. We must teach our female children how to listen to the tides that course through them and our male children how to listen to the cycles that tell them when to work, play, and rest. In this, we can help them understand that they will be listened to more attentively if they themselves can learn how to listen better, for listening enhances communication and relationships. Modeling such an improved way of relating for our children encourages them to help us to create a better world for us all.

As we make these changes, we begin to follow a creative vision for a new way of being in relationship—all relationships.

TECHNIQUES FOR CONSTRUCTIVE CHANGE

As we change the practices upheld by our existing myths, we are creating a new reality. If you are puzzled about how to do this, simply look at what's not working in your life and imagine how it could be different. The imagination is a wonderful tool to dream our way toward action. Once you can see what you want to change, you can start to make it happen. Stop believing in old ideas and accept the wisdom your heart provides to imagine new possibilities. Balance the time you spend in the artificial, technological parallel universe of cell phones and the Internet with time spent in nature, listening to the voice of the divine feminine, and aligning your rhythms with the rhythms of Earth and the cosmos. Inspiration for a better way of living often comes when one spends adequate time in nature.

One night during the time I was exploring separate sleeping during Nature's gift I had a very powerful dream. At the time I was pursuing my Ph.D. in psychology at Saybrook University, and I was in search of an appropriate topic for my dissertation. The dream I had caused me to expand my own exploration of the benefits of secluding myself during menstruation. I designed a research study to examine the experiences of other women who had agreed to sleep separately during their time of flow. The results of this study revealed that women who did so experienced increased creativity, enhanced intuition, more meaningful dreams, and better harmony in their relationships. (The experiment that led to my dissertation is outlined in appendix 1.)

At this juncture, I would like to encourage all of my women readers to take a beginning step—a step on behalf of the health of all women, families, and the planet. I encourage women to slow down from their daily activities and rest during the time that they are bleeding. Listen to your body's clock rather than adhering to society's artificial calendar. Determine what is best for you. Limit the number of things you normally do, and determine for yourself if you want to go to work, or if you need to stay home and rest. I recommend arranging your schedule to allow personal retreat during your cycle whenever possible. Arrange childcare so that you can take care of yourself. Prepare food in advance so you do not have to cook. Or better yet, have someone else cook for you. I encourage men in relationships to adjust your schedules to accommodate your partner's cycle and to support her during this time.

Resting during the time of flow not only gives the physical body a chance to cleanse and heal, it offers the benefit of allowing a woman's attention to gravitate to spiritual planes to resolve problems and gather wisdom. For those who do want to try this form of retreat during Nature's gift, in order to derive spiritual, creative, or relationship benefits, be gentle with your first efforts in this direction. Remember that even if you do not use this sacred cleanse to prepare for new life, retiring to listen to spiritual guidance brings greater harmony overall. Often new ideas, solutions, brainstorms, or inspirations arrive through dreams. Again, the portal is wide open during this time. It is good to be in your own space, free of distracting influences. It also sets an example for men to become aware of their own rhythms and needs for retreat, which they can pursue by meditating, taking a walk, or retreating from society and spending a longer time in nature.

To explore different possibilities for creating a better life, you may want to experiment with setting up your own private sacred space to cleanse, dream, and connect with the divine feminine. Probably you have your own ideas about how to do this. But if you feel unsure, here are a few suggestions. If you have a partner, be sure your partner understands and supports your explorations. It's not helpful to suddenly leave the marital bed without clearly explaining your intention. Additionally, if your partner feels rejected or abandoned, it will be more difficult for you to focus on your own exploration. A thoughtful, kind, and honest explanation can give both of you an opportunity to grow as you explore a new path.

Design your own sacred space to feel comfortable and inspiring to you. Make it inviting and soothing. Include candles, fresh flowers, special art or objects, favorite books, a journal, crayons or paints—whatever you want that inspires you. Add tissues in case you decide you need a good cry. Decorate in colors that encourage inner reflection. Incubate your ideas and emerge from your sacred space with a creative plan to incorporate positive changes in your life. Put yourself first for a change. How can you help all the people who depend on you if you don't take care of yourself first? Rest.

Write your thoughts and feelings in a journal as if you were writing to a special friend. Paint or dance your emotions. Stop the same old arguments you have always had with yourself or with others. Change your beliefs. Give up trying to convince someone else of your viewpoint, and honor the fact that you can be right for yourself alone. Start your own savings account to make your dreams come true. Plan (and then take) the trip you have always wanted to take. (Travel helps to expand one's perspective.) Dream and then acknowledge your dreams—the day and the night kind.

Keep a dream journal by your bed and record the guidance that comes through in your sleep. Color in it. Keep a mood chart and see how often you are peaceful and content. Chart your own rhythms. When do you feel sensitive and quiet? When do you seek the company of others? When do you feel creative? When are you more intuitive? When do you solve problems more easily, and when do problems overwhelm or tire you? When is your sex life the richest? When do you find it easiest to communicate clearly with your partner? With your children? With your friends? At work?

Color your chart and make it a personal reflection of your own inner rhythms. Recognize the ebb and flow of going inward and of wanting to connect. It is a natural gift to have the dual nature of doing both. Learn to be grateful for the times you are more sensitive and cry more easily, for these are windows you can look through to see what is out of balance. Learn to honor the right time for the right action or inaction. PMS and work overload are not excuses to be emotionally out of control. Fully experiencing a retreat does not mean being weak or restricted from doing things.

Again, a sacred retreat is about listening to your inner wisdom to know when is the most appropriate and most effective time to cultivate visions and dreams, to make a special project really work, to help your family and community, to make a difference in the world. Rhythms of life bring change. If we listen well, we can direct these changes to create a better world. Changes on your chart should reflect the changes you are making in your life.

In our modern-day experience of the world, many people believe they are too busy, too distracted, too hungry for something they need, or just too tired to begin to make changes. Some may be simply trying too hard, rather than listening to their intuition and going with the flow of energies that will arrive to support them. It may seem overwhelming to begin to make changes, so I offer a few practical solutions for creating a new reality.

The most valuable suggestion I can offer is that you slow down. Create opportunities to listen deeply. Find your own connection to nature and honor it. Reestablish respect for your own inner rhythms and your connection to Earth's rhythms by going to bed early at night, rather than reading or working late; eating when you are hungry rather than at scheduled times; and resting when your body enters into cycles of purification.

I implore you to simply begin to notice how life is based on cycles. Notice the seasons; notice the moon; notice Venus in the morning and evening sky; notice the trees sprouting or shedding their leaves; notice the cycles within your own moods and relationships. It is only when we begin to notice and understand the nature of cycles in life that we can see how out of balance we have become. Everything is connected, no matter how much we have been deluded by culturally induced narcissistic beliefs. Nature has her own intelligence that is superior to the most brilliant human mind and will, ultimately, refuse to be controlled by humans.

Withdrawing to a quiet space alone on a regular basis gives the divine feminine in all of us a chance to be heard. And a room of our own is not the only, or even necessarily, the preferred, way of creating a sacred space. We can immerse ourselves in the quiet of nature to create a sacred space and balance ourselves internally. The power to bring harmony to the world is born out of these sacred times of solitude. It is within our power to dream up a million ways to make a difference. To reinstate an ancient practice of spiritual retreat requires small steps to gain acceptance in our personal lives first, which hopefully, will then gain respect in modern cultures. It is our sacred responsibility to make time and space to listen to the voice of the divine feminine as she calls us.

THE VOICE OF THE DIVINE FEMININE

One day I was practicing the art of tai chi with a group of friends, outside in nature. Together in silence, we flowed with the gentle movements in a unified rhythm. Suddenly my attention was drawn to a large tree that was sheltering us. A light seemed to be emanating from the tree, and it grew brighter and brighter until it required my complete attention. The next thing I knew I was on the ground, shaking, with my friends gathered around me. I was freezing cold, and my friends were wrapping me in blankets. The look on their faces was not concern, but awe. I was puzzled. As I regained my equilibrium I was told that a very powerful voice had emerged from me, cautioning the group by saying, *"Listen my children, it is time to come together. It is time to stop fighting and to love one another. It is time to see the truth."*

Although everyone in the group told me what I had said, I had no memory of anything except the beautiful white light that had commanded my attention. For some reason, I associated the light with the presence of an energy that I refer to as Mother Mary, one aspect of the divine feminine. I just knew that the divine feminine was making herself present in my life in a way that could not be ignored. This energy I call Mother Mary had literally appeared to me and spoken through me to others. Her message—that it was time to see the truth—left me knowing that personally I was not living an authentic life. At that time my life was defined by the needs and rules of the man to whom I was married, while my own needs were unrecognized and unmet. I was living in an unbalanced situation of service to someone else's life without honoring the importance of my own life or, indeed, without knowing who I really was. The voice of justice roared through Mary's appearance to me, as she told the entire group that it was time to make changes. Soon thereafter, I dissolved my marriage.

After that, I saw Mary's presence a number of times in special circumstances, but it wasn't until many years later that her voice came through me again. By this time I had adjusted to the power of her energy, and I was able to remember what she said. She has not been the only one who has chosen to join her energies to mine to share her messages, but she was the first and the most powerful, and she stays with me to this day, helping and supporting me in myriad ways.

I would like to make it clear that my association with the divine feminine is not a religious association; it is a spiritual one. I recognize the elevated vibration of her energy, and I deeply appreciate what she chooses to share with me. One of the gifts of Mother Mary's presence is helping us to find whatever has been lost (from car keys to our sense of self). Our largest loss is the loss of our connection to nature, to the divine feminine, and to each other. Mother Mary is available to help us find our way and to reconnect us once again.

Mary Magdalene also speaks through me. I experience such fire in the presentation of her energy that the temperature in the room actually rises noticeably. When she speaks to a group, those who are closest to me usually have to remove sweaters or move away from the intensity of the heat she brings with her light. Her messages are always strong reminders to step away from fear and return to love—another way of encouraging us to return to the divine feminine ways of being in the world to find our balance.

Divine feminine energy has been represented by many images and names in different cultures. Mother Mary, Mary Magdalene, Venus, Isis, Ishtar, Guadalupe, Shakti, and Isanklesh are a few. I call this energy "Mary energy" because the energy appears in the form of Mary to me and, to my mind, Mary is the essence of the divine feminine. One can feel her presence as love, for she represents an opening of the heart, and her presence calls us to return to the realization that we ourselves are divine.

Mary calls us to awaken and to reclaim our power as we remember and recognize who we are as divine sparks of light that are connected to the whole. We all wish to live in love, in health, in peace, and in joy. We can no longer allow others to control us, for we are part of the Divine. We can no longer indulge in feelings of being less than or in actions that continually put others first before caring for and loving ourselves. All love begins within us, in our own hearts. Mary calls us to give birth to our true selves and to join the cycles of life from a place of divinity, recognizing the power we hold within our love. The secret is love. We must continually allow love to flow through us, from us, and back into us.

In *The Dream of the Cosmos,* Anne Baring reminds us that "The resurgence of the feminine invites a new planetary consciousness where the deepest instincts of the heart in both men and women—compassion, informed intelligence, and a longing to protect, heal and make whole—are able to find expression in ways that can best be described as devotion to planetary and cosmic life."[1]

While not everyone has a direct experience with the energy of the divine feminine in the form of Mother Mary or Mary Magdalene, the

Mary energy is present in all of us, both women and men. We can see the dual qualities of the divine feminine by simply gazing into the night sky and watching the cycles of Venus. The divine feminine honors, loves, and respects every aspect of the whole, and her call is a call to return to unity—a return to love.

Today the Mary energy is increasing, imploring us to honor the divine feminine in order to heal the imbalances so prevalent in our world. We have misused duality; it was never intended to lead to conflict and separation. Duality was intended to show us the values of other viewpoints and to draw us closer to wholeness. Is it possible that through deepening our understanding of the importance of all life cycles, that we could be the ones who will save the world? No one is going to do it for us—we hold the power of choice. The divine feminine is calling us, and it is up to us to listen and respond.

A plea to listen to the call of the divine feminine is a plea to save our own lives and the life of the planet. It is a plea to return to the wisdom of connection through finally understanding that everything cycles and that all cycles are connected and essential. It is egotistic to believe that humans will always be on Earth. It's possible that if we continue to separate ourselves from nature and the cycles of life that we may eradicate our own species. It's past time for breaking free from patriarchal dogma that has kept us imprisoned in dysfunctional beliefs about who we are and how we relate in the world. It's time that we turn around, look in the opposite direction, and begin to honor and support the voice of the divine feminine as she calls to us to save our world and ourselves.

Thank you for listening, and thank you for doing your part.

APPENDIX 1

The Research

WHILE WORKING to obtain my Ph.D. in the psychology of consciousness, I designed a seven-month study with Western women who had never been exposed to the idea of nighttime sequestration during menstruation. Requirements for participation included that each woman be in a monogamous heterosexual relationship of at least two years' duration, that she be in good health with no known physical or psychological concerns, that she have a room that could be turned into a sacred space for sleeping during menses, and that her partner be supportive of her participation in the research. My research question was, "Does separate sleeping during a woman's menses affect her relationships, her dreams, her creativity, and/or her intuition and spirituality?"

Finding volunteers was more difficult than I had imagined it would be. I posted announcements at health conferences and universities across the country. When I screened applicants, I found some who were interested but had not been with the same partner for the required time, some who had complicating health issues, some who didn't want to sleep separately from their partners, some whose partners did not support their participation, and some who met all other criteria, but had no room in which to create a sacred space. There were more women with reasons not to participate than volunteers who met all the criteria. That in itself was a profound statement about women's misunderstandings of the many benefits of treating menses as a special time.

Finally I had a small but scientifically acceptable number of volunteers in place. What I had intended to be a preliminary study turned out to be groundbreaking work. In examining the extant literature I did not find any other research of this type. The women who participated in my study came from varied backgrounds in terms of their age, level of education, geographical locations they were from, and spiritual practices. Although I preferred to include only women without PMS, it was impossible to do so because, without exception, every woman interviewed answered the question, "Do you have PMS?" in the affirmative. Women who listed only the mildest premenstrual changes, such as bloating, breast swelling, headaches, abnormal appetite or food cravings, fluid retention, acne, or heightened emotions attributed all of these changes to PMS, because they did not understand that increased sensitivities and changes are a normal part of the female cycle.

The protocol for the study required that each woman arrange a sacred space in her house to which she could retire at any time of her choosing and where she would sleep during menses for five months out of a study designed to last for seven months total. In the first and seventh month of the study, each woman slept with her partner, as usual, to provide a baseline of comparison to the five months they slept separately during menses.

Each participant was given a journal and instructed to write or draw in it daily. Any event of significance was to be recorded, including dreams, relationship issues, spiritual experiences, and creative ventures. If nothing significant happened in their lives, they recorded that. The women were also given questionnaires and instructed to fill them out on the first day of bleeding of the first, fourth, and seventh month. Responses were counted and tracked for change over time. Finally each woman was interviewed in the first, fourth, and seventh months, and their partners were interviewed at the end of the study.

My research focused on the cyclical process of women's lives, and the effects of treating menstruation as a sacred time of withdrawal for contemplation and personal processing. Empowering effects were hypothesized for each of the four areas traditionally important in women's lives and community, and deeper connection to spiritual and intuitive guidance.

Below are the questions I posed as part of my research, as well as a brief summary of the results of each question:

1. *Will women who sleep separately during menses experience increased creativity?* The research showed that the women in this study experienced a general increase in overall creativity from the first month to the seventh month, and many of the women began to have a greater urge to create, or developed more creativity toward the end of each menstrual retreat.

2. *Will women who sleep separately during menses experience greater dream recall?* The research showed that all of the women (100 percent) reported greater dream recall over the course of the seven months, increasing each month from the first month of separate sleeping until the end of separate sleeping. Dream recall lessened when they returned to a shared sleeping space. Women who were unaware that they even dreamed were astounded to discover that they not only dreamed, but that they began to remember their dreams during the course of the research.

3. *Will women who sleep separately during menses have more meaningful dreams?* The research also demonstrated that all of the women (100 percent) reported an increase in meaningful dreams during the time of separate sleeping. Most of the women divulged that their most meaningful or powerful dreams occurred during menses or just immediately before menses when they were sleeping separately, although there was some variation. Women who were unaware that they even dreamed at all began to have meaningful dreams that affected their everyday lives. By

the end of the research, they were using these dreams, which they considered spiritual dreams, for guidance. Additionally, 95 percent of the women reported a decrease in dreams or an increase in disturbing dreams when they returned to their shared beds in the seventh month; one woman was stung by a wasp, which she interpreted as an indication that she was sleeping in the wrong place at the wrong time.

4. *Will women who sleep separately during menses have more spiritual experiences?* All of the women reported a keen awareness of their spirituality during the research. Half the women reported being more generally aware of spirituality, while the other half noted a marked increase in their daily spiritual experiences. A third of the women were drawn to issues that were more spiritual in nature. By the end of the research period, all of the women reported that spirituality was a general undercurrent present in every part of daily living. Additionally, every woman reported being more content with life, more aware of and connected to her inner guidance, and having experienced significant changes in her belief system by the end of the research period.

5. *Will women who sleep separately during menses experience increased intuitive experiences?* All the women in the study reported that their intuition increased by the end of the research. Half of the women linked their intuition to incubating creative ideas, which they acted on later. Half of the women connected their increased intuition to an increase in spiritual experiences. A third of the women felt their intuition was stronger during menses, and by the end of the study all of the women reported that their intuition was more active during the entire month.

6. *Will women who sleep separately during menses experience increased relationship harmony?* This question received a resounding, "Yes!" from both participants and their partners. Women who were struggling with long-term unresolved issues reported resolving the problems; women who had experienced

unexpressed anger with their partners for years learned to express their anger and express themselves; partners reported clearer communication; both participants and their partners reported decreased conflict and quicker conflict resolution; sex lives improved; both participants and their partners told stories of increased personal moments, more satisfying intimacy, and a deepening of their relationships. All women said they were glad that they had participated in the research, and many planned to continue the practice of menstrual separation after the research was finalized.

The reason for having three ways of gathering data (journal writing, questionnaire, and interview) was to be sure nothing was left out or misunderstood. For example, one woman who, on the questionnaire, checked "fine" for every question about her relationship, with only good remarks about her spouse, poured out her heart in her journal about being lonely and misunderstood in her marriage. Another woman, who found it difficult to write her feelings in her journal, filled the questionnaire with side comments and remarks about her life.

Quantitative and qualitative data of this research yielded statistically significant results at a p-value of less than 0.03 percent in all four areas of questioning, indicating that my hypotheses had a 97 percent chance of being true.

When I began my research, I did not expect that long-term effects could be seen until more time had passed because it was the first study of its type. However, the effects turned out to be more far-reaching than expected.

My hope by presenting my research in this book is to reinstate the time-honored understanding of the many gifts of being a woman. If we re-create the myths that have contributed to dismissing or controlling women's gifts, we have the potential to change the world.

An abstract of my original research is included below. For those readers who would like more information or verification of constructs presented in this book, you may order my 2001 original dissertation, *Empowering Women through Sacred Menstrual Customs: Effects of Separate Sleeping during Menses on Creativity, Dreaming, Relationships, and Spirituality*. Order from:

> ProQuest
> 300 N. Zeeb Road
> Ann Arbor, MI 48106–1346

Be sure to include title, year of publication (2001), and sponsoring university (Saybrook University), in your request. In the thesis, you will find detailed support of many of the conceptual constructs presented in this work.

Empowering Women through Sacred Menstrual Customs: Effects of Separate Sleeping during Menses on Creativity, Dreaming, Relationships, and Spirituality

ABSTRACT

The effect of treating menses as a sacred time in Western culture was explored based on the practices of multiple ancient indigenous cultures. The research question was, "How does separate sleeping during menses affect creativity, dreaming, relationships, and spirituality/intuition?" Differences in effects between the time of our menses and when we are not menstruating were addressed as well.

This longitudinal and exploratory study, with a multiple baseline component, involved a seven-month intervention with voluntary, separate sleeping during menses for five months, and two control months of non-separate sleeping. Participants also randomly chose another week, when they weren't menstruating, to sleep separately. Initial participants were ten Caucasian women (two later dropped out) of varying age and socioeconomic backgrounds, recruited through advertisements for a study of menstruation.

Assessments were both quantitative and qualitative. In the first, fourth, and seventh months, participants completed questionnaires and took part in in-depth semi-structured interviews; they kept daily journals throughout the study. Partners were interviewed at month seven.

Results included tabulations of questionnaire responses, subscale scores for perceived change in the four study areas, and an overall score that was considered a measure of empowerment. A two-way analysis of variance by ranks for the total score yielded an overall, significant pattern of positive change over the seven study months.

Qualitative findings—based on interviews, journals, and questionnaire content, and typically confirmed by triangulation—illustrated positive growth in all areas over time. There was a trend toward stronger effects during menses than non-menses, especially in augmenting creativity and spirituality/intuition. Associations between areas appeared for enhanced creativity and intuitive guidance, and spirituality and the quality of relationships. There were diminished effects during control periods.

Overall, for all of the women, the practice of separate sleeping evoked deeper levels of understanding of menses, and of themselves. Participants reported enhancement of all areas and increased feelings of empowerment. Additional research can further explore and compare effects during experimental and control conditions. Research challenging cultural assumptions regarding menstruation in contemporary Western culture may open women to new sources of inspiration and growth.

APPENDIX 2

Blood Rituals
around the World

℘

THE WORD *ritual* comes from the Sanskrit word *R'tu,* meaning "any act of magic toward a purpose," and the Sanskrit word *Rita,* meaning "proper course." *R'tu* has a secondary meaning of "menstrual," suggesting that rituals perhaps first began in direct relation to menstruation. Whether or not the first rituals surrounded menstruation, rituals involving blood have been a part of human history since pre-agricultural times. In hunting and gathering societies, both genders regularly came into contact with blood. For a man, blood was lost either in taking another's life in battle or in hunting. For a woman, blood was lost either as her own menstrual blood or in childbirth. Both men and women considered anything to do with blood as dangerous.

A HISTORICAL OVERVIEW

The historical importance of blood repeatedly shows up in art or in depictions of ancient rituals. One example is the ancient Bushmen rock art that shows the Maluti San of Drakensburg, Africa, collapsing in a trance, covered in blood that is pouring from their nostrils. Classic Mayan art is full of bloodletting imagery. The ancient Maya believed that cutting the penis of the king induced a trance and brought the gods into being. Connection between the ritual and the king's contact with the supernatural was clear. The cosmically potent ritual of kings was upheld as a form of menstruation: the king was the mother of the gods because he gave them birth and nourished them through his gift of blood.

Today we know that chemicals produced by the brain in response to a massive blood loss (a form of endorphins) can induce hallucinogenic experiences. The Maya may not have understood how it worked, but they knew that drawing large amounts of blood would, without the help of other drugs, produce the visions they sought in their rituals. Through these bloodletting rituals and visions, the Maya brought the supernatural realm into the world of man.

Subincision—slitting the penis along its length so that blood can drip over the man's lower body—is still practiced today in Papua New Guinea, Australia, the Philippines, and Africa. These cultures hold the belief that the blood flowing from the wound is no longer the man's blood but becomes sacred women's blood through ritual. Today Wogeo men of Papua New Guinea understand that women are automatically cleansed by menstruation. Since men do not have this automatic process, they periodically incise the penis and allow some blood to flow to cleanse themselves and to guard against potential illness. The Murngin and Dwoma of Papua New Guinea also use this practice for cleansing. In each culture, this process is called men's menstruation.

Historically, there were many parallel menstrual-like rites of seclusion and privation for Native American hunters prior to a hunting excursion, including special instruction by women elders, imitation of menstrual taboos, and induced visionary states. The men in tribal cultures modeled their own rituals as much as possible after women's rituals. A man coming back from war, where he had seen blood, was not considered dangerous. However, he was often given a ceremony for cleansing and peace of mind. Today North American indigenous men participate in river plunges or sweat lodges for cleansing, acknowledging that ritual bleeding is for women only. Indigenous men view their own blood as less perilous than women's blood, which is still considered powerful and dangerous.

Although men's rituals have historically attracted interest, in many cultures men have not even been privy to women's rituals, and when they were, there was generally great respect for them. Only Western patriarchal society has adopted the belief that women's rituals were something forced upon women by men. This misunderstanding comes, perhaps, from a truth outwardly denied by Christian European men: they knew the power inherent in women's bleeding and they intentionally set about to control that power by belittling it.

Other cultures throughout the world have varying approaches to rituals around blood. Some have no rituals for women; others offer rituals for the particular female and her entire family. In Japan, when a young woman begins her period, family and friends are invited for a celebration. While no reason for the celebration is given, candied fruit presented on a tray gives a symbolic message everyone understands that they are celebrating the girl's newly achieved ability to "bear fruit."

Cultures vary in deciding whether rituals are appropriate only at the first menses or are to be continued every time a woman is menstruating. In most Earth-based cultures the world over, the first period is of such importance that it is accompanied by rites announcing that the girl-child has earned a woman's place in society. The seclusion of the menstruating girl from the tribe offers an opportunity for various women elders to explain to her the meaning and importance of ritual and what her responsibilities will be as a woman.

THE CONNECTION BETWEEN SPIRITUALITY AND POWER

Historically, indigenous women understood the connection between spirituality and the power available during the bleeding times of their cycles. Although women could not avoid physical dangers brought on by menstruation and childbirth, they knew they could gain spiritual understanding and spiritual power at these times.

As mentioned earlier, in the Cherokee culture, menstruation and childbirth were always associated with spiritual power. Menstruating women in particular were considered to have great power, and men regarded them as dangerous—they were sacred because they were dangerous and dangerous because they were sacred. The Kolish Indians of Alaska confined pubescent girls in a tiny hut, completely blocked except for one small air hole, for one year, during which time they were allowed no fire, no exercise, and no company. The Kolish believed that this type of seclusion forced the young girl to go into a meditative state, since she could do nothing else. She learned how to listen to spiritual guidance and carried that wisdom with her for life.

As we have established, listening for intuitive or spiritual guidance during Nature's gift can bring information for a woman herself or information for a larger community. However, in some indigenous cultures it was understood that some insights gleaned during menstrual listening were only for the woman experiencing the time of flow. She could act on her wisdom, but she would not share what she had learned. Other insights may have been appropriate for sharing with others, bringing creative solutions back to her family or to the community.

Yurok grandmothers taught young women that the potential for spiritual accomplishment was brought on by the power of menstrual blood. They believed that this special time should not be wasted in mundane tasks and social distractions. Instead, all of a woman's energy should be invested in listening to accumulate spiritual understanding of what was required for their lives.

Menstrual blood is considered a gift by the Pygmies in central Africa where the entire community gratefully and joyously receives the gift with festivity. The girl who has reached menarche goes into seclusion, taking all her young friends with her. There, an older woman relative teaches them the arts and crafts of motherhood. A celebration lasting a month or two follows, and friends come from near and far to pay their respects.

In West Central Africa, Akan custom requires that a female who menstruates for the first time come out of her house at dawn crying. She then informs her mother, who gives her a white stool of honor on which to sit at the entrance of the house. The mother announces the news to the community, and older women assemble to sing special songs. The girl plants a peregun tree in the yard of her parents' home. The mother pours wine to the spirits to ask for blessings for the girl. Next, her hair is ritually shaved and preserved, symbolizing the death of her old state of life and rebirth into a new life. She is taken to the riverside, where a young girl and a young boy stand on her left and right, respectively. All three are immersed in the river three times, symbolizing the beginning, middle, and end of life and the appreciation for the future birth of either a boy or a girl. White clay is smeared on the girl's forehead, and she is taken home with her head covered. She is offered mashed yam three times, and she lets the food fall to the floor three times. Finally, a whole egg is touched to her mouth, which she rejects twice and swallows whole on the third time, signifying fertility and life.

In the indigenous Arunta and Ilpirra tribes of Australia, a mother takes her daughter at first menstruation to a spot close to the women's camp, to which no man ever goes. The mother makes a fire and a camp and instructs the girl to dig a hole about a foot to eighteen inches deep. The girl then sits over this hole attended by her own mother and some other tribal mothers. During the first two days her task is to sit over the hole without stirring or leaving; after that she may be taken out to hunt food by one of the old women. When the flow ceases she is told to fill the hole. She now becomes what is called *Wunpai*. She returns to the women's camp, and shortly afterward undergoes the rite of opening the vulva and is handed over to the man to whom she has been bespoken.

Ritual similarities exist between these present-day Australian Arunta and ancient North American Anishinabek. In the past, young

Anishinabek women at menarche went to a specific cave that was shaped like a vagina; it was understood to be the vagina of the Earth. There the girls sat listening to the nearby creek, making the connection between the flow of their own bodies' blood and the flowing of the blood of the Earth. This is a connection worthy of remembering for all of us, women and men alike. If we had more respect for the flow of women's blood and the understandings connected to it, we would, perhaps, also have more respect for the Earth.

Neither Earth's cycles, nor women's, need to be controlled. Each contains a natural power that supports the correct timing of life and death. Possibly it is the recognition that women understand that everything has a correct timing, and that death is part of the order, that causes so much fear and results in the cultural desire to control feminine cycles. If we understand that death comes when the time is right, we stand in the way of the men who defy death and seek to control who lives and who dies. Looking at the world through wholly male eyes, we see an unending string of acts of death portrayed by the patriarchy as supporting life: trees are cut and animals are slaughtered in their prime; wars are waged and lives are taken to preserve someone else's view of how life should be lived. Feminine views and understandings promote all of life and a weaving and balancing of everything and everyone. Everything is connected, and the natural cycles of life and death are well understood.

OTHER ABORIGINAL AND INDIGENOUS RITES RELATED TO MENSTRUATION

In Aboriginal tribal life, an older female such as an aunt or grandmother, ritually guides young women through the initiatory experiences of menstruation and childbirth. For several months the young woman is covered with mud, smoked with special leaves, and able to eat only the food brought to her by her older female initiator. No sweets such as honey are allowed for four moons. After some time, the women of the tribe make her a camp closer to the big camp. At that time she is painted with red ochre and white gypsum and her arms and head are adorned with sprays of sweet-smelling white flowers. White swans' down is scattered over her head, and a sprig of a sacred tree is placed through the hole in the septum of her nose. The older woman gives her a bouquet of smoking leaves to carry as she walks toward the main camp. As she walks, the other women sing her songs in a strange language.

The young woman then encounters her betrothed husband sitting on a log with his back to her. As the singing builds in momentum and pitch, the young girl hurls her bouquet to the ground, grabs her betrothed husband by the shoulders, and shakes him. She then runs away. In a few weeks time, she is shifted again to a camp closer to the main camp. A fire is made for her, on the other side of which her betrothed husband is camped. This gradual bringing together of the couple increases the dramatic intensity and mystery surrounding their inevitable union.

The young couple camps like this for one moon, at the conclusion of which the old woman informs the young girl that it is time to camp on the same side as her husband as his wife. He is required to treat her well, or her relatives will take her from him. If we had such rituals in Western culture, courtships that honor natural timing and require respect from both parties, with the support of family and community, would our divorce rate be as high as it presently is?

Anishinabek girls are immediately taken into the bush when their first menses begin. The girl makes a small shelter where she will stay until her bleeding stops. Her mother returns with necessities for her temporary residence. Each day a female elder spends the day with her, imparting knowledge and sharing the wisdom she will need as an adult. She fasts for seven days. Girls usually have vision-dreams during this fast that empower them for the rest of their lives. The period of isolation is called *makwa* or "turning into a bear." The bear is a powerful healing spirit, closely connected with Earth. At the end of the fast, the girl, now a woman, washes herself and her clothes and walks on a bed of cedar boughs for purification, then goes home for a ritual feast.

Among the Diné, *kinaalda,* meaning "'blessing way ceremony,'" is performed for a young girl in honor of her first menses. Young girls in their first (or second) menstruations are considered to have a unique power that can bring positive effects to her family and tribe. To maximize these effects, families prepare for the moment that the girl will inform her mother that her first menstrual period has begun. The bleeding is considered a sacred ceremony bringing blessings, and a blanket is hung over the hogan, signifying that a ceremony is in progress. Blessing way songs are sung among the Diné for the girl's first menses in order to counteract any danger to her or others who may be present. Legends of the first kinaalda tell the story of the girl running in joy on her own for four days, making up a new song each day. The songs give her energy and prepare her for her existence. She runs with the songs in all four directions.

Following the legend of the first kinaalda, a new Diné menstruant runs for four days, in the early morning, into good fortune. After running as far as she can, she stretches out her arms and takes four deep breaths, drawing in the dawn air with her arms each time. Then she bends down, touches Mother Earth, and blesses herself by applying moist soil to her body from her feet upward. Some of the reproductive power possessed by her during her first and second menses is transferred back to Mother Earth through this process. The final step in the ceremony after she runs and sings for four days is to be painted in white paint in recognition of the fact that she is symbolically the holy Diné Changing Woman. After her four-day ceremony, the young girl washes her hair, ritually pouring the water in the hogan near the door. Then she retires to reflect on her ceremony and her learning for four more days.

The Mescalero Apache Girls' Puberty Ceremony occurs once a year for all young girls who have started their menses in the past year. The ceremony celebrates the transition from a girl's adolescence into woman-hood. It is an elaborate four-day public event wherein male singers sing sixty-four different songs on each of the four nights. There is feasting, present giving, and dancing. It is believed that this ceremony insures the survival of the people. (This four-day public ceremony is followed by a four-day private ceremony.)

The first menstrual flow of each Apache girl is celebrated through this joint ritual, wherein each girl is honored by the people as a tempo-rary manifestation of the female deity Isanaklesh. It is a proud day for the girls' families, who recognize the divinity now present in the power of bringing forth life. Each girl is placed in her own tipi before dawn and carefully bathed and dressed for the ceremony. A mentor reminds her of how good it feels to be cared for; this helps prepare the girl to care for others. This instilling of the idea that one must care for oneself well in order to know how to care for others well is a beautiful and meaningful inspiration that engenders true abilities to care for others as oneself.

While all this is happening, the girl's male kin construct a sacred tipi on ceremonial grounds. From there the power of the ceremonial songs will go out to all the people on Earth. The ceremony's songs, sacred narratives, and images combine to make a powerful imprint of the deity on both the girl and her attending relatives and friends. Knowing that, at night, male dancers will appear to bless her, for four days the girl allows only close relatives, friends, or those who wish to be blessed into her tipi. Then, for four more days, the girl secludes herself in order to reflect on her ritual experience. There is a feast following the last day of the ceremony.

In many indigenous tribes including the Cherokee, the Yurok, the Diné, and the Apache, women and men are considered to have oppo-sitional (or opposite) powers. Oppositional powers are not considered positive versus negative, but simply different, like cold versus hot. The principle of oppositional powers is obvious when one looks at nature. Everything in nature has an opposite: cold and hot, day and night, summer and winter. In many indigenous belief systems, women are considered cold and men hot. The extra cold (and wet) of a woman's menstrual cycle can put out the hot (and dry) fire of a man's energy. Indigenous women knew that they were so powerful they could potentially overwhelm a male's power. Because of this, they chose to stay away from men during the time of flow so as not to harm their men's opposite powers. In *Walking in the Sacred Manner: Healers, Dreamers, and Pipe Carriers—Medicine Women of the Plains Indians,* the husband and wife ceremonial research team Mark St. Pierre and Tilda Long Soldier express the principle of opposites as told to them by the late Joseph Rockboy (1900–1984), a revered Yankton/Sicangu Sioux elder:

> A woman is the only one who can bring a child into this world. It is the most sacred and powerful of all mysteries. . . .
>
> When a woman is having her time, her blood is flowing, and this blood is full of the mysterious powers that are related to childbearing. At this time she is particularly powerful. To bring a child into this world is the most powerful thing in creation. A man's power is nothing compared to this, and he can do nothing compared to it. We respect that power. . . .
>
> You see, a woman's power and a man's are opposites—not in a bad way, but in a good way.
>
> Because of the power a woman has during this time, it is best that, out of respect for her men and for their medicine things, she stay away from them. In the past they would build a little lodge for her, and their other female relatives would serve on her needs. She would get a rest from all her chores. It was not a negative thing like people think now. So you see, we did this out of respect for this great mystery, out of respect for the special powers of women.[1]

Blood rituals also mark the end of menses. Female companions of Tiwi women of Melville Island in Australia paint a red stripe down the front of a woman's body when her menstrual flow begins, symbolizing a snake. She is then led to another camp where her male relatives and her future husband wait for her. A ceremonial spear is briefly placed between her legs and then presented to her intended husband, who hugs the spear, calling it wife. The girl's father places a palm tree upright in the ground and an elaborate game begins where the girl runs from her intended until he catches her. The husband-to-be and his brothers dance around her and women wash her, repaint her, and place feathered ornaments on her. She is then presented to her husband, but they are not allowed to talk to each other and she sleeps on the opposite side of the fire from him every night until her menstrual flow is over. The next morning the husband paints his wife. As he does so, they may talk to each other, and wedded life begins.

As mentioned earlier in the book, Cherokee women follow a ritual at the end of every menses, plunging seven times in a river and changing their clothes before going home. This plunge in running water removes anything that might harm their community and brings them what they need to take back to their community. The Cherokee plunge, used this way, is an extension of a purification ritual that both men and women perform as a daily morning practice.

North American indigenous women have held rituals for every menses and for every birth. Ogallala girls wrap up their first menstrual flow and put it in a tree to impart positive influences to them throughout their lives. Zuni women perform ceremonies to celebrate the sex of their babies: A large seed-filled gourd is placed over a female baby with spoken prayers that her sexual parts grow large and her fruit abundant. A boy baby's penis is sprinkled with water as prayers are said, asking that it remain small, implying that women's life-bearing capacity is immense in comparison to that of men. The act of hair brushing, viewed as a rite of purification following first menses, exists today as a female ritual, although it has lost its original meaning.

Today few blood rituals designed by and for women exist in the modern world. In some cultures today it is the men who, according to their religion or beliefs, proclaim what is to be done with bleeding women. Islamic women are secluded during menses, according to Islamic instructions that have ritualistic overtones allegedly derived from the Qur'an. Until they have ceased menstruating and purified themselves, women are not allowed to participate in public worship. Orthodox Jewish women follow the same purification laws.

Sadly, in America, there are no rituals for menstruating girls or women, and the entire affair is treated as a scientific biological event or something to be ignored or dismissed as interfering with normal progress. The modern world could learn much from the community blood rituals of the Diné and other Earth-based peoples that teach respect as well as how to care for ourselves in order to care well for others.

THE WEST'S WAY
OF BEING IN THE WORLD

Western Christian culture has offered us two diametrically opposite ways of being in the world, neither of which is balanced. Patriarchal values have taught us to look out for number one (ourselves) at the expense of everyone else. Christianity has taught women to sacrifice themselves for the good of others. Christian doctrine teaches that we are all sinners, and as such, are unworthy. Children are confused by a world that offers a choice of selfish taking and altruistic giving, with no instructions or insights as to the relationship between the two. Somewhere between family of origin teachings and cultural values, each person decides how they are going to operate in the world. Those who choose (either consciously or from survival needs) to be caregivers would benefit greatly from learning to care for themselves before they offer care to others. Workshops and other forms of support exist to teach burned-out caregivers the art of caring for themselves, but unfortunately, lifetime habits and ideas are difficult to change.

The dichotomy of values inherent in Western culture causes a deep rift between people—a cultural split between people who focus on selfishness, and caregivers who understand that we are all connected. Because there is little training on how to care for ourselves (as opposed to selfishly looking out only for ourselves), there is a true lack of balance between caring for ourselves and offering care to others. Caregivers suffer greatly in our culture from an inability to give the same loving care to themselves as they offer to everybody else.

A return to meaningful rituals surrounding the cycles of our lives would honor the return of the divine feminine, where everything is respected as part of the whole.

Taboos Surrounding Menstruation

BECAUSE OF THE INTENSE beliefs about blood, particularly menstrual blood, it easily follows that some sort of rules were needed to contain or control the power contained in blood. These rules defined certain things one was not allowed to do at certain times. The English word *taboo* comes from the root *ta*, meaning "to mark," and *pu*, which means "intensity." In Polynesian culture the root words are combined together to form *tapua*, meaning both "sacred" and "menstruation."

The most commonly found taboos across cultures have to do with menstruation. Women who understood the power contained in the mysteries of menstruation originally created taboos around it. When men understood that women had the power to create life—a power that was connected to menstruation—they began to fear it because it was also connected to death.

Thus men, wishing to control women's power, changed the women's taboos and expanded them. Throughout history, taboos surrounding menstruation developed into laws that were enforced, sometimes to the point of death. The patriarchy was born and further reinforced when men decided to try to take away the power of women by forbidding them to participate in previously meaningful community activities.

DID TABOOS ABOUT MENSTRUATION ORIGINATE WITH THE CHRISTIAN CHURCH?

The origination of taboos is marked with controversy, and I contend that the Christian Church was a very big player in their origin and implementation. It created a myth that spelled out the danger of listening to women's wisdom and punishing women for bringing forth life. Bearing in mind the fact that most early research on taboos was done by men, it is not surprising to find a universal myth of the toothed vagina as a source of an incredible number of taboos on menstrual blood. The toothed vagina is symbolic of a recognized power held in the blood, capable of harming a man.

Taboos originating prior to the founding of the Christian Church can be traced to sacred observations leading to practices designed by women for women, practices women imposed on themselves and on men for the protection of all. Some anthropologists even went so far as to recognize that menstrual taboos indicated a superior status of women. For example, in Portugal women set menstrual taboos in place because it allowed them to control certain social interactions and gave them a rationale for protecting the economic privacy of their homes, for which they held primary responsibility.

It's interesting to note that taboos surrounding menstruation originally restricted the behaviors of others more than the behaviors of the menstruating woman herself until the advent of Christianity. Each woman chose to seclude herself and avoid others. Interfering with her choice to remove herself from daily activities and interaction with others was forbidden. Patriarchal rules derived from Judeo-Christian ethics and Muslim ethics twisted the original taboos of protection into taboos formed by new myths where women were seen as unclean temptresses to be strictly avoided. Through both Muslim and Judeo-Christian teachings, beliefs about menstruation as a powerful vehicle for change went underground. Menstruation became something to be hidden, something shameful. Today, if a woman is menstruating and seen as unapproachable, it is no longer because of her stance of power, but because of a taint placed upon her by the religion of her culture. No wonder it has taken modern women so long to publicly acknowledge the importance of one of their most primary bodily functions.

SEPARATION TABOOS, AND TABOOS PERTAINING TO FOOD AND FIRE

Separation taboos came into place for reasons already explained—to protect others from the potentially dangerous energy that surrounds the discharge of women's life-bearing blood. Prior to Christianity, taboos were devised to contain women's energies and keep them from spreading beyond a limited place in the order of things. Early menstrual taboos included separate sleeping during menses, food restrictions (including the fire that cooks food), non-touching, and avoidance of water and sunlight. The reason for separation, unfortunately, was twisted, until women became segregated with the stigma of being tainted or soiled themselves and less holy than the men who condemned them. After the installation of Christian values the danger that came with women's monthly power was treated as something to restrict rather than respect.

The custom of separation taboos, early isolation of menstruating women, often in special shelters, was widespread in Earth-based cultures. Yurok women did not sleep with their husbands during menstruation, nor engage in any regular daily activities. Menstruating women in the Algonquian-speaking people of Labrador separated themselves in ceremony, sitting in an area sacred to women, opposite their husbands. This was an indication of separate but equal gender positions.

In many indigenous practices, ritual separation during Nature's gift begins when a girl has her first menses. Thus she begins her marriage with the idea that menstruation is her sacred time and withdraws accordingly. Additionally, many indigenous societies have built-in social support that allows someone else in the family or community to take over a woman's duties during her time of flow so that she can retire. Finally, many indigenous tribes have a cultural understanding of the underlying implications of a woman's power and how withdrawing during menses is appropriate for a woman's own inner work, inspiration, and guidance for her community.

As previously mentioned, most tribes held the belief that until a young girl learned how to control her energy it could be very dangerous. So her grandmother took her to sacred women's lodges and taught her the ways of this special time. Cherokee people acknowledged that a husband was affected by the power his wife was experiencing during her time of flow because of the nature of their relationship. Therefore menstrual restrictions extended from her to him. Under no circumstances would a menstruating woman or her husband participate in a public ceremony.

Menstrual taboos around food and fire began before the advent of language. In *The Woman's Encyclopedia of Myths and Secrets,* renowned historian Barbara Walker refers to ancient myths about collective sex strikes orchestrated by the women of each tribe, who synchronized their monthly cycles to force the men to hunt for food. The absence of food combined with the prohibition against sex encouraged men to go off and hunt. The taboo against a woman's approaching a cooking fire makes sense if we remember that during menstruation a woman may be discharging powerful emotions. Such emotions could energetically harm another (those eating the food for example) with disruptive energy.

Additionally, menstruation itself represents water and cold. Fire is hot. Water puts out fire, so why would an intelligent menstruating woman want to challenge the fire that cooks her family's food with the presence of her own very potent moisture? Even today, among many Earth-based tribes, abstaining from cooking and/or approaching a cooking fire is a taboo that menstruating women observe. The Beng of the Ivory Coast, for instance, do not cook or touch logs or coals of a fire while they are menstruating. Menstruating women of the Australian Arunta tribe do not gather the irriakura bulbs, a staple of their diet, lest the bulbs fail. Cherokee and Malekula women do not farm, cook, or care for children during menstruation, nor do their husbands.

Certain tribes worldwide have restrictions regarding the touching of certain, or all, foods during menstruation. According to the Anishinabek, berries are linked to the blood of the Earth, so they are considered too powerful for a young girl to eat at a time when her own female powers are developing.

With the arrival of Christianity in ancient Europe (and later in America) time-honored food and fire taboos were twisted to demean menstruating women. In Rome, menstruating women were avoided because of fables that they could turn wine sour, make crops barren, gardens dry, fruits fall off trees, hives of bees die, mirrors dim, and iron rust. Even today in Italy, Spain, Germany, and Holland, peasants believe that flowers and fruit trees will wither from contact with a menstruating woman. The only difference in ancient and modern food taboos is the attitude, which has been colored from one of respect to one of rejection.

TABOOS RELATED TO TOUCH, WATER, AND EARTH

Other common ancient menstrual taboos concerned touch. Sensual awareness was replaced by spiritual focus during menstruation, so any type of touch was believed to distract from a woman's inner awareness. In many indigenous cultures, no one was allowed to touch a menstruating woman, nor would she touch herself or anyone else. Even scratching one's own skin or hair was prohibited during menstruation.

The Yurok believe that one should feel all of the body exactly as it is and pay attention to what it has to tell you. Therefore, rather than scratching absent-mindedly with their fingers, they use a scratching implement. This facilitates a focus on the body by making even the most natural and spontaneous of actions fully conscious and intentional. The taboo of non-touch during menses was used to gain spiritual power. The discipline required to keep this taboo helped to create a person with strong mental concentration and great control of her own body.

The issue of power kept the taboo of non-touch in place in most cultures. The Gimi of the Eastern Highlands in Papua New Guinea believed menstruating women had such power that their touch would cause wooden bowls to crack, and stone axes to misbehave in the hands of their male owners, inflicting otherwise inexplicable wounds upon them. It was not only taboo to touch the living; sometimes this taboo extended to the dead. Among the Beng of the Ivory Coast, menstruating women are restricted from touching a corpse. Since the menstruating woman symbolizes fertility, she should not have close contact with a corpse, which is a symbol of death. Clearly this prohibition was in place to protect women.

Like touch, food, and fire restrictions, there were also taboos around water and earth. During menstruation, the Beng would not set foot in the forest. The Carrier Indians carried young menstruants from point to point to keep their power separate from the earth. The Tiwi of North Australia believed a young girl's first bleeding caused her to be particularly vulnerable, and she honored many taboos for her own protection.

The separation from water and earth probably came from a mythic belief that if menstrual blood mingled with Earth-blood (water), all of Creation might unravel. Following this belief, menstruating women lifted the veil between one reality and another with the awareness inherent in the blood of life they carried and released through their bodies.

Following the separation from water and earth, menstrual lodges and sanctuaries were among the first features relinquished by native people upon Christian-European contact. While one might speculate that forced relocation of indigenous peoples by Europeans made it more difficult to maintain separate sleeping spaces for menstruating women, the more likely reason for the elimination of sanctified treatment of menstruating women (or all women) was that the treatment of menses in Christian-European patriarchal cultures was clearly different and more demeaning.

The wisdom councils of many Native American tribes were actually made of women, who convened to discuss important issues, and from their discussions determined the actions the male chiefs would take for the benefit of the entire tribe. To conquer a powerful people, as all Earth-based people were, the Christian-Europeans began by disempowering the women. It could be said that the largest loss leading to the downfall of Native Americans in the United States was the loss of acknowledgment of their women's power. When that was displaced, it was easy to unbalance the culture and conquer the men. Men are nothing without the balance of women, and the same can be said for women; we need each other to be balanced. Now that you understand how and why menstrual taboos were set in place, I trust each woman reading this work can find her own set of taboos to support and honor her own inner wisdom.

Notes

CHAPTER 1.
THE CYCLIC NATURE OF LIFE

1. Thoreau, *The Journal,* 225.
2. Eliade, *Myth of the Eternal Return,* 87.
3. Conrad, coursework, 2000–2009; Pert, *Molecules of Emotion.*

CHAPTER 2.
BIOLOGY AND HEALING

1. Ford, *Listening to Your Hormones,* 61.
2. Vliet, *Screaming to Be Heard,* 35.
3. Sichel and Driscoll, *Women's Moods,* 79.
4. For instance, see Teramoto, Ioki, Rutkowska, and Tokura, "Daily Rhythms in the Core Temperature"; Kim and Tokura, "Preferred Room Temperature Self-Selected by Women"; Turek, "Circadian Rhythms"; Trickey, *Women, Hormones and the Menstrual Cycle;* Brien, Martin, and Bonner, "Tryptophan Metabolism during the Menstrual Cycle"; Severino, Bucci, and Creelman, "Cyclical Changes in Emotional Information Processing in Sleep and Dreams"; Metcalf and Livesey, "Distribution of Positive Moods in Women."
5. Conrad, personal correspondence, 2000–2009.

CHAPTER 3.
RELIGION REPLACES SPIRITUALITY

1. Flinders, *Rebalancing the World,* 71.
2. Ibid.

3. Baring, *Dream of the Cosmos,* 153–54.

4. St. Pierre and Long Soldier, *Walking in the Sacred Manner,* 74–75.

5. Yousafzai, *I Am Malala,* 24. See also Syed and Ozbilgin, *Managing Cultural Diversity in Asia,* 112.

6. Baring, *Dream of the Cosmos,* 176.

CHAPTER 4.
BLOOD MYSTERIES

1. Conrad, personal correspondence, 2000–2009.

2. Allen, *Sacred Hoop,* 47.

3. Paper, *Through the Earth Darkly,* 173.

4. Cohn, "Sex and Death in the Rational World of Defense Intellectuals," 687–718.

CHAPTER 7.
DEEP LISTENING

1. Ogden, *Heart and Soul of Sex,* 30.

2. Kornfield, *A Path with Heart,* 171.

CHAPTER 8.
RELATIONSHIPS OF THE HEART

1. Ogden, *Heart and Soul of Sex,* 30.

2. Shuttle and Redgrove, *The Wise Wound,* 21.

CHAPTER 9.
DREAMING CYCLES

1. Krippner, "A 10-Facet Model of Dreaming."

2. Achterberg, *Woman as Healer,* 27.

CHAPTER 10.
CREATIVITY CYCLES

1. Krippner, "Creativity and Dreams," 597–606.

2. Anderson, *Therapy and the Arts,* xii.

3. Richards, "The Subtle Attraction," 195–237.

4. May, *Courage to Create,* 38.

5. Runco and Richards, *Eminent Creativity.*

6. Ibid.

7. Weiner, *Geography of Genius,* 198.

CHAPTER 11.
MENOPAUSE MAGIC AND
ANDROPAUSE AWAKENING

1. Northrup, *Women's Bodies, Women's Wisdom,* 4–5.

2. Platt, *Adrenaline Dominance,* xi.

3. Northrup, *Wisdom of Menopause,* 19.

CHAPTER 12.
THE WATER WE ARE

1. Gardner, *Experimenting with Water,* 25.

2. Marks, *Holy Order of Water,* 192.

3. Schwenk, *Sensitive Chaos,* 41.

4. Conrad, *Life on Land,* 321.

CHAPTER 13.
WELCOMING THE DIVINE FEMININE

1. Baring, *Dream of the Cosmos,* 221.

APPENDIX 2.
BLOOD RITUALS AROUND THE WORLD

1. St. Pierre and Long Soldier, *Walking in the Sacred Manner,* 74–75.

Bibliography

Achterberg, Jeanne. *Woman as Healer.* Boston: Shambala, 1991.

Allen, Paula Gunn. *The Sacred Hoop: Recovering the Feminine in American Indian Traditions.* Boston: Beacon Press, 1992.

Anderson, W. E., ed. *Therapy and the Arts.* New York: HarperCollins, 1977.

Baker, Robin, ed. *The Mystery of Migration.* New York: Viking Press, 1980.

Baring, Anne. *The Dream of the Cosmos: A Quest for the Soul.* Dorset, England: Archive Publishing, 2013.

Berry, Thomas. *The Dream of the Earth.* San Francisco: Sierra Club Books, 1988.

———. *Evening Thoughts.* San Francisco: Sierra Club Books, 2006.

Bettelheim, Bruno. *Symbolic Wounds: Puberty Rites and the Envious Male.* New York: Collier Books, 1955.

Brien, S., C. Martin, and A. Bonner. "Tryptophan Metabolism during the Menstrual Cycle." *Biological Rhythm Research* 28 (1997): 391–403.

Briffault, Robert. *The Mothers.* New York: MacMillan, 1927.

Buckley, Thomas, and Alma Gottlieb. *Blood Magic: The Anthropology of Menstruation.* Berkeley: University of California Press, 1988.

Campbell, Joseph. *Myths, Dreams, and Religion.* New York: E. P. Dutton and Company, 1970.

Campbell Joseph (Library of). *Goddesses: Mysteries of the Feminine Divine.* San Francisco: New World Library, 2013.

Capra, Fritz. *The Web of Life.* New York: Doubleday, 1996.

Cohn, Carol. "Sex and Death in the Rational World of Defense Intellectuals." *Signs* 12, no. 4 (Summer 1987): 687–718.

Conrad, Emilie. *Life on Land.* Berkeley: North Atlantic Books, 2007.

Coveney, Peter, and Roger Highfield. *The Arrow of Time.* New York: Ballantine Books, 1990.

Csikszentmihalyi, Mikhael. *Flow: The Psychology of Optimal Experience.* New York: Harper Perennial, 1990.

Delaney, Janice, Mary Luptton, and Emily Toth. *The Curse: A Cultural History of Menstruation.* New York: E. P. Dutton and Company, 1976.

de Losa, Patty. "Marion Woodman and the Search for the Conscious Feminine." *Parabola,* Spring 2016, 60–67.

Dreyer, Ronnie Gale. *Venus: The Evolution of the Goddess and Her Planet.* San Francisco: Aquarian Press, 1994.

Eliade, Mircea. *The Myth of the Eternal Return: Or, Cosmos and History.* Princeton, N.J.: Princeton University Press, 1971.

Flinders, Carol Lee. *Rebalancing the World: Why Women Belong and Men Compete and How to Restore the Ancient Equilibrium.* New York: HarperSanFrancisco, 2002.

Ford, Gillian. *Listening to Your Hormones.* Rocklin, Calif.: Prima Publishing, 1996.

Frazer, J. G. *The Golden Bough: A Study in Magic and Religion.* New York: MacMillan, 1963.

Frisbie, C. J. *Kinaalda: A Study of the Navaho Girl's Puberty Ceremony.* Salt Lake City: University of Utah Press, 1967.

Gainsburg, Adam. *The Light of Venus: Embracing Your Deeper Feminine, Empowering Our Shared Future.* Burke, Va.: Soulsign Publishing, 2012.

———. *The Soul's Desire for Wholeness.* Burke, Va.: Soulsign Publishing, 2005.

Gardner, Howard. *Creating Minds.* New York: Harper-Collins, 1993.

Gardner, Robert. *Experimenting with Water.* Dover, England: Dover Publications, 2004.

George, Demetra. *Mysteries of the Dark Moon.* San Francisco: Harper Collins Publishers, 1992.

Gilligan, Carol. *In a Different Voice: Psychological Theory and Women's Development.* Cambridge, Mass.: Harvard University Press, 1982.

Goldbeter, Albert. *Biochemical Oscillations and Cellular Rhythms.* Cambridge, Mass.: Cambridge University Press, 1996.

Golub, Sharon. *Lifting the Curse of Menstruation.* New York: Harrington Park Press, 1985.

Gould, S. J. *Time's Arrow, Time's Cycle.* Cambridge, Mass.: Harvard University Press, 1987.

Grahn, Judy. *Blood, Bread, and Roses: How Menstruation Created the World.* Boston: Beacon Press, 1993.

Guttman, Arielle. *Venus Star Rising: A New Cosmology for the 21st Century.* Santa Fe, N.Mex.: Sophia Venus Productions, 2010.

Hobson, J. A. *The Dreaming Brain.* New York: Basic Books, 1977.

Hunter, Kelly M. *Living Lilith: Four Dimensions of the Cosmic Feminine.* Bournemouth, England: The Wessex Astrologer, 2009.

Ingerman, Sandra. *Medicine for the Earth: How to Transform Personal and Environmental Toxins.* New York: Three Rivers Press, 2000.

———. *Walking in Light.* Boulder, Colo.: Sounds True, 2014.

Kahn, Tamam. "Mothers of Islam." *Parabola,* Spring 2016, 54–59.

Kim, H. E., and H. Tokura. "Preferred Room Temperature Self-Selected by Women under the Influence of the Menstrual Cycle and Time of Day." *Biological Rhythm Research* 28 (1997): 417–21.

Knight, Christopher. *Blood Relations: Menstruation and the Origins of Culture.* New Haven, Conn.: Yale University Press, 1991.

Kornfield, Jack. *A Path with Heart: A Guide through the Perils and Promises of Spiritual Life.* New York: Bantam Books, 1993.

Krippner, Stanley. "Creativity and Dreams." *Encyclopedia of Creativity.* Edited by Mark Runco and S. Pritzker. San Diego, Calif.: Academic Press, 2009.

———. *Extraordinary Dreams and How to Work With Them.* New York: State University of New York Press, 2002.

Krippner, Stanley, and April Thompson. "A 10-Facet Model of Dreaming Applied to Dream Practices of Sixteen Native American Cultural Groups." *Dreaming* 6, no. 2: 71–96.

Krippner, Stanley, and David Feinstein. *The Mythic Path: Discovering the Guiding Star.* New York: Jeremy Tarcher, 1997.

Madden, C. C. *A Room of Her Own.* New York: Clarkson Potter Publishers, 1997.

Marks, William. *The Holy Order of Water.* Herndon, Va.: Bell Pond Books, 2001.

May, Rollo. *The Courage to Create.* New York: Bantam Books, 1975.

Metcalf, M. G., and J. H. Livesey. "Distribution of Positive Moods in Women with the Premenstrual Syndrome and in Normal Women. *Journal of Psychosomatic Research* 39 (1995): 609–18.

Montague, Ashley. *The Natural Superiority of Women.* Walnut Creek, Calif.: AltaMira Press, 1999.

Moore, Michael. *Where to Invade Next* (Film). Beverly Hills, Calif.: North End Productions, 2015.

Neuman, Erich. *The Great Mother.* Princeton, N.J.: Princeton University Press, 1963.

Northrup, Christiane. *The Wisdom of Menopause.* New York: Bantam Books, 2011.

———. *Women's Bodies, Women's Wisdom: Creating Physical and Emotional Health and Healing.* New York: Bantam Books, 2010.

Ogden, Gina. *The Heart and Soul of Sex.* Boston: Trumpeter Books, 2006.

Orleane, Pia. *Empowering Women through Sacred Menstrual Customs: Effects of Separate Sleeping during Menses on Creativity, Dreaming, Relationships, and Spirituality.* Ann Arbor, Mich.: Pro Quest Dissertations, 2001.

Orleane, Pia, and Cullen Baird Smith. *Conversations with Laarkmaa: A Pleiadian View of the New Reality.* Santa Fe, N.Mex.: Onewater Press, 2015.

———. *Remembering Who We Are: Laarkmaa's Guidance on Healing the Human Condition.* Santa Fe, N.Mex.: Onewater Press, 2015.

Owen, Laura. *Her Blood Is Gold: Celebrating the Power of Menstruation.* San Francisco: Harper Collins, 1993.

Paper, Jordan. *Through the Earth Darkly: Female Spirituality in Comparative Perspective.* New York: Continuum International Publishing Group, 1997.

Parker, K. L., ed. *Wise Women of the Dreamtime.* Rochester, Vt.: Inner Traditions, 1993.

Perdue, Theda. *Cherokee Women: Gender and Culture Change, 1700–1835.* Lincoln: University of Nebraska Press, 1998.

Pert, C. B. *Molecules of Emotion.* New York: Scribner, 1997.

Platt, Michael. *Adrenaline Dominance: A Revolutionary Approach to Wellness.* Rancho Mirage, Calif.: Clancy Lane Publishing, 2014.

———. *The Miracle of Bio-Identical Hormones.* Rancho Mirage, Calif.: Clancy Lane Publishing, 2008.

Rako, Susan. *The Hormone of Desire.* New York: Harmony Books, 1996.

Richards, Ruth. "The Subtle Attraction: Beauty as a Force in Awareness, Creativity, and Survival." In *Affect, Creative Experience, and Psychological Adjustment.* Edited by S. W. Russ. Philadelphia: Brunner/Mazel, 1999.

Runco, Mark, and Ruth Richards, eds. *Eminent Creativity, Everyday Creativity, and Health.* Greenwich, Conn.: Ablex Publishing, 2009.

Schwartz, M. T. *Molded in the Image of Changing Woman.* Tucson, Ariz.: University of Arizona Press, 1997.

Schwenk, Theodor. *Sensitive Chaos.* Hernon, Va.: Steiner Books, 1998.

Severino, S. K., W. Bucci, and M. L. Creelman. "Cyclical Changes in Emotional Information Processing in Sleep and Dreams." *Journal of the American Academy of Psychoanalysis* 17 (1989): 555–77.

Shuttle, Penelope, and Peter Redgrove. *The Wise Wound: The Myths, Realities, and Meanings of Menstruation.* New York: Bantam Books, 1988.

Sichel, Deborah, and Jeanne Driscoll. *Women's Moods.* New York: William Morrow and Company, 1999.

St. Pierre, Mark, and Tilda Long Soldier. *Walking in the Sacred Manner: Healers, Dreamers, and Pipe Carriers—Medicine Women of the Plains Indians.* New York: Touchstone Press, 1995.

Steiner, Franz Baermann. *Taboo.* Harmondsworth, England: Penguin, 1954.

Syed, Jawad, and Mustafa F. Ozbilgin, eds. *Managing Cultural Diversity in Asia.* Gloucestershire, UK: Edward Elgar Publishing, Ltd., 2010.

Tate, Karen, ed. *Voices of the Sacred Feminine.* Winchester, UK: Change Makers Books, 2014.

Teramoto, Y., I. Ioki, D. Rutkowska, and H. Tokura. "The Daily Rhythms in the Core Temperature during Spring and Autumn under Natural Conditions in Young Women." *Biological Rhythm Research* 28 (1997): 161–65.

Thoreau, Henry David. *Civil Disobedience.* New York: Classic Books America, 2009.

———. Edited by Damion Searls. *The Journal, 1837–1861: Henry David Thoreau.* New York: New York Review of Books, 2009.

Trickey, R. *Women, Hormones and the Menstrual Cycle.* New South Wales, Australia: Allen and Unwin, 1998.

Trinkaus, Emily. "Venus, Mary Magdalene, and the Re-emerging Sacred Feminine." *The Mountain Astrologer,* no. 180 (2015).

Turek, F. W. "Circadian Rhythms: Fascinating Biology." *Biological Rhythm Research* 12 (1997): 299–300.

Vaughan-Lee, Llewellyn. "Reclaiming the Feminine Mystery of Creation." *Parabola,* Spring 2016, 16–25.

———. *The Return of the Feminine and the World Soul.* Point Reyes, Calif.: The Golden Sufi Center, 2009.

Vliet, E. L. *Screaming to Be Heard.* New York: M. Evans and Company, 1995.

Walker, Barbara. *The Woman's Encyclopedia of Myths and Secrets.* San Francisco, Calif.: Harper Collins, 1983.

Weiner, Eric. *The Geography of Genius.* New York: Simon and Schuster, 2016.

Williamson, Marianne. *A Woman's Worth.* New York: Ballantine, 1993.

Woodman, Marion. *Conscious Femininity*. Toronto, Canada: Inner City Books, 1993.

——. *Dancing in the Flames: The Dark Goddess in the Transformation of Consciousness*. Boston: Shambhala, 1996.

Yousafzai, Malala. *I Am Malala*. New York: Little Brown and Company, 2013.

Index